ENCYCLOPEDIA OF **APPLIQUE**

Heather F. Jensen

Heather F. Jensen

Encyclopedia
of
APPLIQUE

An Illustrated, Numerical
Index to Traditional
and Modern Patterns

Barbara Brackman

EPM

Publications, Inc.
McLean, Virginia

Library of Congress Cataloging-in-Publication Data

Brackman, Barbara.
    Encyclopedia of applique : an illustrated, numerical index to
traditional and modern patterns / Barbara Brackman.
      p. cm.
    Includes index.
    ISBN 0-939009-75-7
    1. Appliqué—Patterns.   I. Title.
TT779.B73   1993
746.44'5041—dc20
                                                   93-34626
                                                   CIP

EPM Publications, Inc., 1003 Turkey Run Road,
  McLean, VA 22101
Printed in the United States of America

Cover and Book Design by Tom Huestis

Contents

Preface

*"It is not wise
to be didactic about the nomenclature
of quilt patterns."*

FLORENCE PETO, *American Quilts and Coverlets.* 1949, pg. 21.

This is my second index to quilt design. The first, *An Encyclopedia of Pieced Quilt Patterns* grew to eight volumes and 4000 designs drawn from patterns published between 1835 and 1980. I had long resisted indexing applique because the patterns seemed so diverse and unclassifiable. Applique did not appear to follow the geometric structures of pieced designs. The technique itself allowed much freedom to the individual quiltmaker who could move leaves, stems and flowers around at will, creating designs quite different from her model. Applique designs imitate nature with its seemingly infinite variety and thus seem infinite themselves. But nature has been categorized into species and genus, so why shouldn't appliqued designs also fall into categories?

The majority of the patterns included in this index were published in books, periodicals and pattern company catalogs. I have read dozens of sources published from 1835 through 1992 but found most applique designs in print after 1920. During the nineteenth century, commercial sources rarely included applique designs, so some common designs and many uncommon ones were not recorded in print. Because a significant aspect of applique design would be missed if I referenced only published patterns, I also indexed designs I have found in quilts. I focused that research on appliqued album quilts with dates actually inscribed on them, so most of unnamed patterns described as "from an album" will be followed by the date inscribed on the quilt. I did not include many designs that originated after 1960.

The index is designed to enable you to find the name of an unknown pattern. But keep in mind that the names are highly arbitrary. We know very little about what nineteenth-century quiltmakers called their quilts. By the turn of the twentieth century when the periodicals started recording names, the whims of the editors and designers were often the source for the names. Most of the names you will find in this index are names used by people born after 1900.

I used to believe that every pattern had a name, and with persistence I could find it. After spending the last 15 years or so surrounded by index cards with drawings and tiny photocopied clippings, I am now ready to agree with Florence Peto's caution about names.

I could not have done this book without the assistance of many friends and correspondents. First I want to thank Cuesta Benberry and Joyce Gross for sharing their knowledge and their libraries. I am grateful also to other members of the American Quilt Study Group for their answers to my questions. And many thanks to researchers who indexed applique before I started to try to sort it all out—among them: Jeana Kimball and Elly Sienkiewicz for their work with nineteenth–century applique designs; Louise Townsend for her index to *Kansas City Star* patterns; Wilene Smith for answers on a number of pattern sources, especially Nancy Page; Merikay Waldvogel for her index to Anne Orr; Yvonne Khin and Judy Rehmel whose books have served as my applique resources for years; Edna Van Das for her amazing index to the Nancy Cabot patterns, and Wilma Smith for her indexes to practically everyone, especially the prodigious Laura Wheeler.

***Calendula** or **Allen Rose** by Rose Good Kretsinger (1886–1963), Emporia, Kansas, 1930–1932. Collection of the Helen F. Spencer Museum of Art, University of Kansas. Gift of Mary Kretsinger. This masterpiece of stuffed quilting and applique is an updated copy of a mid-nineteenth-century quilt owned by the Allen family. The names are Kretsinger's; the patterns are variations of the floral numbered 18 and the wreath numbered 173 in the Index.*

PART 1

INTRODUCTION

"As American as Applique"

If the quilt is the quintessential American folk art, applique is the characteristic American quilt. The applique quilt, so typical in America, is unusual elsewhere. Although needleworkers in many other cultures have decorated cloth by applying layers of fabric and some have combined the technique with quilting, the red and green American quilt with its distinctive repeat of floral forms is unique.

Like much else in our culture, the applique quilt is a recipe for the melting pot. Beginning with a stock of English bedding traditions, quilters added substantial parts of German design and contemporary decorative arts. They spiced the mix with images from diverse immigrant and native folk arts.

European and African traditions of decorative applique date back centuries. During the Renaissance in western Europe, the technique was used to ornament liturgical vestments and hangings, as well as secular clothing, bedding and draperies. Never as common as woven or added thread decoration, it was considered a type of embroidery, known as intarsia embroidery (Italian for inlay or encrust) and was most prevalent in Italy, Spain and France. Quilt historians Marie Webster and Schuppe Von Gwinner noted numerous examples of applique from the African continent. John Vlach, an expert on African and African-American arts, has directed American eyes to the traditional applique hangings of several African regions, particularly Benin (formerly Dahomey), and asked provocative questions about the transmission of design ideas.[1] Most of the applique designs on bedcovers and hangings from Europe and Africa are pictorial narratives, with religious, patriotic or military themes, but among the pictures of warriors, royalty, animals and mythical figures are floral and geometric designs much like American motifs.

Left. *An embroidered figure of a Mano chief, Liberia, Africa. Before 1945.*

Right. *A block from an appliqued wallhanging of the Fon tribe, Benin, Africa. Ca. 1900.*

Applique combined with quilting is less common in old world cultures. Von Gwinner pinpoints the oldest surviving applique quilt as Swedish, attributed to 1303. She pictures another Swedish quilt, made a century later, which anticipates many characteristics of American quilts. Appliqued in repetitive blocks, it features stylized animals inside roundels (circles) from which four fleur-de-lis sprout.[2]

Motifs drawn from a Swedish quilt, 15th century.

Several examples of appliqued bedcovers and quilts survive from eight-eenth–century Germany (not then a country but a group of independent states united by a common language). Like English and American quilts from the same time period, German applique was often based on a medallion format with a central design focus, usually a large block surrounded by fields of patchwork.

The Rise of The Conventional Applique Technique

American seamstresses initially favored a type of applique quilt that is now called *Broderie Perse* (French for Persian Embroidery), in which the decorative elements are cut from a printed chintz and appliqued to a plain ground. The technique has been traced to seventeenth-century Europe when the first printed chintzes became popular there.[3] Numerous eighteenth-century examples sur-

Motifs drawn from a an appliqued quilt dated 1779, southeastern Germany. Although many, such as the one on the right, have little to do with American applique, the pot of flowers with the eight-lobed rosette bears evidence of German roots for American applique.

vive in England, and it is likely that the technique for making *Broderie Perse* quilts came to America with the English taste for chintzes.

Several American quilts and bedcovers dating to the last quarter of the eighteenth century are decorated with applique cut from chintz. The style was popular enough in the early nineteenth century that English and American mills printed chintzes with figures designed to be cut out and stitched onto quilt tops.

Chintz applique quilts made in America between 1750 and 1840 share several design conventions, including a medallion format framed with rows of borders. The designs had an Oriental lushness because the chintzes from which they were cut were heavily influenced by European interpretation of Asian art. Major themes were the flowering tree (the tree of life) and a central vase holding many blooms, which were true-to-life depictions of peonies, chrysanthemums and roses. Color schemes were naturalistic greens, reds, browns and yellows. The flowers were commonly cut from fabric with a white ground and rearranged on another white ground.

Broderie Perse, according to needlework historian Susan Burrows Swan, is a late–nineteenth–century name for an older technique. An early published use is in Caulfeild and Saward's 1882 English needlework book in which they distinguish between "true applique with plain colord stuffs" and "broderie perse," also called "applique with cretonne" (a synonym for chintz).[4] During the century or so that cut-out chintz dominated American applique, seamstresses sometimes included motifs in the former technique. They constructed designs of plain fabrics or small-scale prints, a technique known today only as "applique." To distinguish between techniques, I have referred to the applique technique we use today as "conventional applique" because so many patterns were called Conventional Rose or Conventional Tulip and because the technique is now the conventional method.

Detail of a cut-out chintz or **Broderie Perse** *applique, ca. 1800.*

Detail of a quilt in the conventional applique technique, ca. 1840. Smithsonian Institution Negative 75-15211

Between 1775 and 1840, quiltmakers most often used conventional applique in borders or as secondary motifs to accent the major designs cut from chintz. An occasional woman used conventional applique exclusively. Eagle designs were favorites; some of the first block-style applique were variations of the Reel pattern with several examples dated in the 1810–1830 period (see patterns numbered 17.1 and 17.2).

Conventional applique blossomed about 1840. The subordinate technique abruptly became the primary decoration, completely replacing cut-out chintz within a few decades. By the time Caulfeild and Saward described cretonne applique in 1882, it had almost disappeared in the U.S., succeeded by a taste for the cleaner lines and formalized shapes of the conventional applique.

After 1840, block patterns exploded in diverse, sophisticated design with no gradual evolution from the simple to the complex. Most of the traditional patterns in this index can be traced to the first years of the style; few originated after 1865 and the end of the Civil War. It wasn't until twentieth-century pattern designers began reshaping applique that we see another burst of innovative design.

The reasons for the genesis of conventional applique are many. They include changes in fashion, fabric and technology and cultural adaptations. There is some evidence that the technique was popular here in the 1840s for clothing and other textiles. Georgiana Brown Harbeson, who wrote on American needlework, noted the fashion for appliqued ladies' cloaks in the 1840s and 50s.[5] She also quoted *The Lady's Work Box Companion*, circa 1850, which stated "Applique, combined with embroidery was much in vogue a few years since, particularly for handscreens, where the flowers and leaves were formed of velvet and the stalks embroidered with gold bullion." A similar pamphlet entitled *The Lady's Guide to Embroidery and Applique* said, "applique is one of the most beautiful, and at the same time one of the easiest modes of embroidery and may be worked with great rapidity."[6] These manuals, although "revised and enlarged" by American women, were probably direct copies of English material, as were most other needlework publications of the period. Their meager patterns and descriptions of materials have more in common with intarsia embroidery than with American quilts, yet the sewing techniques are similar.

If applique decorations were popular for clothing and household decorations, it would follow that girls learned the skill through patchwork. Textile historian Virginia Gunn, who has noted the commonalities in nineteenth-century quilts and clothing, hypothesizes that techniques such as the whipped seams found in template patchwork, corded binding, and the straight seams pressed to one side typical of piecework seams are components of quilts because quilts served as samplers for children's needlework training.[7] Teachers might well have taught applique as it became an important decorative detail.

Fashion in home interiors of the middle and upper classes underwent a change in the first half of the nineteenth century. Jack Larkin, in *The Reshaping of Everyday Life 1790-1840*, discusses the absence of ornamental possessions in the average home early in the century. He quotes an 1828 letter from Margaret Hall who, awed by the luxuries in a South Carolina plantation, focused on "snow white quilts and draperies."[8] By the 1840s these items were far more common in the homes of a growing middle class.

Even the bedrooms of those wealthy enough to afford draperies underwent a change in the 1830s. The typical American bed had been enclosed in hangings for privacy and warmth, but changes in fabrics and taste began to dictate open beds. Ideas about health also affected style as people adopted a belief in the benefits of a fresh breeze. Bed hangings were thought to encourage miasmas (bad air that caused illness). Applique quilts and other striking new types of bedding provided the decorative emphasis on a bed without hangings.

Two quiltmaking fashions that bloomed during the 1840s are entwined with the changes in applique. The block quilt replaced the medallion format as the major American style. The calicos and plain fabrics required for conventional applique were more suited to repetitive quilt blocks than was traditional chintz with its limited number of repeats that could be cut. As the album or friendship quilt became a fad in states from Maine south to the Carolinas and west to Ohio, the freedom of conventional applique meant that each donor to the group project could personalize her contribution.

Fashion is often dictated by changes in technology. In analyzing quiltmaking trends one must always look to trends in fabric production. In the early nineteenth century, American mills, learning to compete with English and French cotton manufacturers, offered prints at prices that democratized fabric. Calicos at 10 to 40 cents per yard meant that families of working men or women who themselves worked could afford the cotton for a new dress or a quilt. New Hampshire school teacher Elizabeth Hodgdon, who earned $11 in 1832 for 11 weeks of teaching, was certainly cash poor by our standards, but in her account book she recorded an expenditure for 8 yards of calico at 14 cents per yard.[9]

The new, lower price of calicos consequently democratized quiltmaking, enabling more American girls and women to take up the craft that had been the domain of the well-to-do for centuries. As cheaper calicos replaced the more expensive chintzes, conventional applique replaced chintz applique.

The lower price of fabric also freed women from home textile production. No longer required to spin and weave, the average woman could devote her time to patchwork with purchased cotton. Even the mechanization of the pinmaking industry probably affected the popularity of the applique technique, which requires much preparatory basting or pinning. Before 1840, most American pins were imported. The 1832 invention of an American pinmaking machine meant a significant decrease in the price of a paper of pins, further democratizing certain needlework techniques.

An important influence on the new look in applique quilts was the adoption by the Pennsylvania Germans of the bedding of their neighbors of British ancestry. The Pennsylvania Germans (often called the Pennsylvania Dutch) were descendants of immigrants from many of the German-speaking states who settled in southeastern Pennsylvania between 1683 and 1820. Primarily farmers and artisans, they were Protestants of the Lutheran and Reformed congregations. (Amish and other sectarians formed about 10% of their numbers.) Slow to assimilate American culture, they continued to speak German, continued to work crafts such as furniture and metalwork in German style, and made their beds in German fashion, sleeping under heavy ticks, more like feather beds than comforters. While their English-American neighbors patched quilts and wove coverlets and blankets, generation after generation of Pennsylvania Germans persisted in filling home-woven ticks with straw and feathers.

Jeannette Lasansky, a Pennsylvania folklorist, has noted that Pennsylvania German dowry records, wills and estates began listing quilts about 1830, evidence of the period when they adopted the form of the three-layer bedcover fastened with a quilting stitch.[10] Surviving quilts from mid-century Pennsylvania German families indicate they also adopted the standard English and American pieced patterns—stars, checks and wheels. They did not, however, take up the *Broderie Perse* technique, but preferred applique designs based on traditional German folk art motifs. They replaced the Chinese-inspired tree of life with three geometric flowers in a pot and the Persian chrysanthemum with an eight-lobed rosette, motifs that dominated American applique for the rest of the century.

Design Sources

Despite their diversity, applique patterns fall within certain structures, as folk arts usually do. The majority of the nineteenth-century designs have a four-way mirror-image symmetry with four identical quadrants. Many designs feature a central motif with radiating units. Exceptions include blocks such as baskets, urns and bouquets with two-way symmetry.

Most of the classic applique motifs indexed in this book—the standards that look so American to the quilt lover's eye—can be traced for centuries in European cultures. Carnations, peonies, pineapples, feathers and simple rosettes featuring four, five and six lobes are common in Jacobean embroidery, the English style that goes back to the days of King James I in the sixteenth century.

Other applique designs reflect nineteenth–century fashions in ornament. Grapes and grape leaves, eagles, wreaths, rising suns and fleurs-de-lis decorated all manner of American objects.

Motifs drawn from an embroidered bedspread made in 1772 that exemplifies the English Jacobean traditions in needlework design.

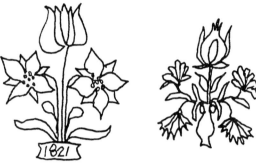

Motifs drawn from Pennsylvania German crafts. The pot on the left is incised in a plate dated 1821; the pot on the right is painted on a chest ca. 1830.

The Germanic tradition is most apparent in the eight-lobed rosette and the three-lobed tulip, the two most popular elements in floral quilt patterns. Reinhard Peesch, an historian of European folk art, describes the rose that quilters call the Rose of Sharon as more a metaphor than a natural flower and notes its relationship to the eight-pointed star, often used in German folk arts and American quilts to represent a flower with stems and leaves.[11] Although simple rosettes with four, five and six lobes are common in decorative arts from Jacobean embroidery to the beadwork of the Great Lakes Indians through cowboy boots in the 1940s, it is the eight-lobed rosette that dominates in both German folk arts and nineteenth–century American applique. Had applique designs developed directly from English and French needlework traditions without Germanic influence, there would be far more emphasis on four- and five-lobed rosettes than we find in quilts made after 1840. Had needlework and ornament from the popular culture of that era affected quilt design, we would see far more emphasis on realistic roses, pansies and lilies found in the Berlin work (needlepoint) that was so fashionable during the golden age of applique.

Rosettes and tulips are not the only design ideas that traditional German ornament and American applique share. Peesch describes potted flowers, usually featuring a "stem with three sprouting blooms" growing out of a vessel with two slim handles. In addition to roses and tulips, the pots often sprout carnations with fan-like crowns, an image less common in American quilts than in German ornament or Jacobean embroidery. Peesch also describes the pomegranate, a round fruit with many seeds visible through an oval incision. A similar motif is often called the Love Apple in American quilt design. Other categories in Peesch's index of German folk design include the paired couple, the magic knot (an interlaced knot) the Basque cross (similar to a swastika), the heart, the eagle, and the Garden of Eden, images repeated in many variations in American applique.[12]

A comparison of American applique designs to Germanic folk arts reveals numerous similarities that are more than coincidence. It is likely that American applique developed when the Pennsylvania Germans adopted the bedding of the English Americans and translated the decorative motifs to their own design vocabulary. The Pennsylvania Germans, living in the area that cultural geographers identify as the central midlands, have had the same strong influence on the applique quilt that they have had on other folkways from coverlet weaving to barn architecture.[13]

Of course, some standard patterns in American quilt designs go beyond the conventionalized motifs of the Pennsylvania Germans. Between 1846 and 1852, the women of Baltimore and surrounding counties developed a style of applique that was quite luxuriant and naturalistic. Few of their elaborate patterns were repeated outside the area. Many seem to be the whim of an individual or a brief fashion among a small group.

Two quilt patterns that are unique to regions of the United States. Variations of the twin cornucopia and dove are from the Baltimore vicinity between 1840 and 1860; the medallion is found in the Carolinas in last half of the nineteenth century.

This photo appeared on a stereo-card about 1900. Whether she is making an applique block or an embroidered piece, she is following her pattern intently.

Southern quiltmakers also developed distinctive applique designs not seen in the central midlands or midwest. Idiosyncratic designs have been traced to specific regions of the Carolinas, Kentucky and Tennessee. These few patterns remained unique to the area because these states sent fewer cultural traditions on the western highways than did the central midlands.

The color scheme for applique quilts was as conventionalized as the patterns. The two standard combinations were blue print calico on plain white grounds or red and green on white. Between 1840 and the Civil War, the red was usually a Turkey red calico, dyed in a lengthy process that produced an unusually fast and brilliant red dotted with paisley cones, florets and geometric figures of blue, green, yellow, black or white. Plain red cottons became increasingly popular in the 1850s. By the last quarter of the century, reds for applique were nearly always plain fabrics.

The green cottons that formed the leaves were either printed or plain and, in mid-century, overdyed— first colored blue and then yellow or vice versa. The two-step process eventually resulted in the fading of one dye or the other, leaving yellow-green or blue-green leaves. Popular accent shades were vivid double-pink prints, chrome yellow and chrome orange (a shade of yellow-orange).

The popularity of red and green on white seems likely to have been a combination of function and fashion. The choice of white for the large background areas was undoubtedly a practical matter; undyed cotton was cheaper than calicos. Turkey red, although expensive, was unusually stable in an era of unstable dyes. And the green, though it did fade, faded in an acceptable manner. The colors also reflected the shades of nature and those in the long-popular, naturalistic chintzes. Red and green had been a traditional color scheme with Pennsylvania German folk artists working in other media, more evidence of their influence.[14]

The classic blue and white color scheme seems to have been strongly influenced by indigo blue and white woven coverlets, which were also common bedding at the time. The blue cottons in the applique quilts were nearly always printed with small white geometrics and the dark blue was probably dyed with the colorfast indigo. Like Turkey red, indigo blue was more expensive but worth the price.

Changes in Applique Style

The years 1840 to 1880 were the prime of the applique quilt, with those made in the first twenty-five years generally the finest. Post-Civil War quiltmakers were less inclined to add delicate details and fine quilting, especially stuffed work, to their quilts. Thus, quilts made after 1865 tend to lack the elegance of pre-war masterpieces.

Regional differences in style, as well as in pattern, developed throughout the decades. No other group of quilters can claim so distinctive a style as the pre-war Baltimore Album artists, but more subtle preferences for pattern, contrast and color combinations did rise and fall. The postwar textile industry brought new Southern mills which produced few of the calicos in which the northern mills had specialized. Thus postwar applique artists in the South confined themselves to plains rather than prints. At the risk of overgeneralizing about regional styles, I will say that postwar Southerners who made applique quilts also showed a strong preference for straight set blocks rather than diagonally set blocks, for contrasting sashing and for simple patterns, with tulips— either single or four set in a mirror-image repeat—especially popular.

During the last decades of the century, quilters in southeastern Pennsylvania where the Pennsylvania German influence is greatest developed a regional style based on color. They appliqued designs to figured grounds, producing unusually colorful quilts with bright blue or yellow print subsituting for the traditional neutral white.

Because the western migration from the area had slowed, this regional style did not spread to quilters in other areas.

Pattern Sources

"December 17, 1835. We attended the fair of St. Andrew's Church. The Council Chamber of the City Hall was tastefully decorated with evergreen, artificial flowers, etc. The variety of articles was much reduced, the prettiest having been disposed of. . .I bought a. . .pattern card for patchwork."[15]

With rare exceptions such as Phoebe George Bradford (1794-1840) of Wilmington, Delaware, who wrote the above in her diary, nineteenth-century diarists and letter writers were silent about where they found their quilt pat-

Applique pattern cut from a sewing machine catalog, ca. 1890. Found in Lancaster County, Pennsylvania.

terns. One is tempted to believe that each applique artist followed her own creative vision, but my experience in classifying applique designs has taught me that a one-of-a-kind applique quilt is rare indeed. The many duplicates indicate that patterns were passed around in some fashion. Especially strong evidence of this are pairs or groups of quilts that are similar in sashing, border and quilting, as well as in the choice of pattern.

Quilters now obtain their patterns on paper—either bound into books and magazines or unbound "in the sheet." Pattern cards like the one Phoebe Bradford bought at the church bazaar have not survived nor have any mid-nineteenth century patterns in the sheet. Bound patterns for quilts, pieced or applique, were rare until the 1890s. Those periodicals or needlework guides that did publish patterns derived their designs from England by plagiarizing British publications. Consequently, the few applique patterns published here between 1840 and 1885 have little to do with American quilts. By the time published patterns were widely available, interest in applique had waned, so it isn't until the revival of applique in the 1920s that we see an extensive body of applique designs in print.

Nineteenth-century quiltmakers were versed in many forms of needlework and probably used similar methods to obtain patterns for embroidery, quilting and patchwork. Needleworkers have had pattern books available for centuries. Davida Tenenbaum Deutsch, in an article entitled "Needlework Patterns and Their Use in America," lists books published in Germany, the Netherlands, Italy, France and England during the early sixteenth century.[16] Pennsylvania-German embroiderers often copied their traditional designs from graphed patterns, which could easily be adapted to applique work.[17] The German patterns on gridded paper probably reached an audience of quiltmakers beyond south-eastern Pennsylvania, one way the German design influence may have diffused so thoroughly into American culture.

Deutsch also notes the importance of sewing curricula published in several American cities to teach poor girls needlework skills. Prominent were Lancasterian needlework instruction books named for Joseph Lancaster (1778-1838) who developed the idea in England. The Baltimore school book, published in 1821, included illustrations and instructions for various designs. The book published in Albany, New York, suggested teachers create a pattern book "with handsome specimins (sic) for the imitation of scholars." Although Deutsch mentions no applique designs, several of the embroidery patterns are easily adapted to applique. One can also imagine that needlework teachers taught applique using standard patterns in the same way they taught embroidery. Each may have developed her own distinctive appliqued designs or used versions published by others.[18]

In the mid-nineteenth century, professional artists in many fields sold their own hand-drawn patterns to handcrafters with less design skill. Phoebe Bradford's pattern card may have been hand drawn by a talented church member. Such a scenario might explain the similarities in the extraordinary Baltimore Album blocks.

Some of the designs unique to the Baltimore quilts are related to theorem (stencil painting), a craft popular with women in the second quarter of the nineteenth century. Painting teachers designed and sold stencils for theorems to their students. *Art Recreations*, an 1860 book, instructed women in the techniques of making their own theorem stencils and advised them that the craft was "better adapted to fruits, birds and butterflies, than to landscapes and heads."[19] Theorem conventions emphasized still life designs with fruit-laden compotes and baskets full of flowers, many of which resemble the patterns numbered 42.6.

Motifs drawn from a theorem painting on the left and an 1848 album quilt on the right.

Few original stencils for theorems survive, but it is obvious that they were in wide circulation during the years of the fad. Theorem painters cut stencils from what was called horn paper, a stiff, waterproof material made by coating pasteboard with linseed oil and turpentine.[20] Cultured young women, trained to produce horn paper, stencils and theorems, could easily transfer those skills to patchwork patterns.

Craftsmen also used stencils to decorate furniture, tin ware, walls and floors. Many of the designs popular with Pennsylvania German stencillers are similar to classic applique designs. It is easy to imagine how a quiltmaker might appropriate a stencil and pass it to her friends, spreading Pennsylvania German motifs into her community and beyond.

There is also a minor tradition of stencilled quilts and spreads. The few that survive are attributed to the years 1825-1835.[21] If these attributions are correct the stencilled spread is a forerunner of the conventional applique quilt. The transition from painted floral design to applique would be a simple process.

Many applique artists probably made their own patterns. Techniques for copying designs directly from another textile were common knowledge to mid-nineteenth century women. In 1830, *Godey's Lady's Book* instructed seamstresses to take rubbings from needlework they wanted to copy by fixing a sheet atop the piece and rubbing the surface with nutmeg, a technique that would work well with applique.[22] The *Arts Companion,* published in 1749, described a tracing technique: "By the help of a Window, or a Glass held up to the Light, we copy all sorts of Prints, Designs and other pieces, upon Paper or Vellum, by fixing them to the paper or vellum we would draw upon. This is an easy and very good Contrivance for copying of the same size."[23] Once she traced or rubbed a pattern onto paper, the seamstress could prick the lines with a pin. Laying the paper atop her fabric, she "pounced" the design by sprinkling a powder that sifted through the pinpricks onto the fabric. She could reuse the paper pattern for each of the blocks in an applique quilt and pass it on to admiring friends and relatives.

Quilt patterns used by Mrs. Erastus Bissell in Ohio in the second quarter of the nineteenth century. Ruth Finley saved her grandmother's quilt patterns and photographed them for her book, **Old Patchwork Quilts and the Women Who Made Them**. *In the book she described them as being of mill net. The material feels very much like the starched net we had in our crinolines of the 1950s. Although the patterns were used for quilting designs, patterns like this could easily be adapted for applique.*

There is much evidence that patterns were stored and circulated in the form of fabric blocks, which could also be traced or rubbed for duplication.[24] These fabric patterns survive as single blocks or as part of sampler quilts. The tradition of cloth patterns continued after the advent of pattern companies. The Ladies Art Company gave customers a choice of paper patterns or fabric blocks well into the 20th century.

Pattern Names and Terminology

Nineteenth-century women were far less descriptive about their quilts in their diaries and letters than today's quilt historians would wish. I have read well over 100 such documents and found no descriptions of the applique technique, no terms for it and precious few references descriptive enough to allow one even to guess what kind of quilt was in process. More helpful than most is Emily Hawley Gillespie's entry in her diary: "March 14, 1861. Piece on a quilt. Have 28 blocks done."[25]

Diarists, when they mentioned their quilts at all, described them in terms of fabric or color, rarely technique or pattern. Typical is Elizabeth Porter Phelps. "April 19, 1767. Wednesday came here Miss Penn and Miss Polly to help me quilt a dark brown quilt..." Seventy years later, Pamela Brown wrote: "April 12, 1837. Pieced a bed quilt of old calico." And Chastina Rix described her work: "September 22, 1849. Helped Sarah quilt, on her pink and white quilt like mine."[26]

The sparseness of their descriptions indicates that names for specific patterns, whether pieced or applique, were unimportant if they were used at all. However there are intriguing exceptions. Elizabeth Myer wrote a letter in 1859 describing a "Flowering Almond" and left a quilt to her descendants much like the "Flowering Almond" numbered 16.65 in the index. In 1847 Parnel R. Grumly inscribed "The Peony and Prairie Flower No. 6" on the back of her quilt and in 1855 Jane Shelby wrote "Mississippi Beauty" on the back of hers. Elizabeth Range Miller left a "Rose of Sharon" in her 1857 will.[27]

Once we realize how little we know of nineteenth-century pattern names, the question of the "right" name for a pattern becomes moot. Arguments about the accuracy of "Princess Feather" versus "Prince's Feather" are absurd. There are no correct names for traditional quilt patterns; oral tradition changes, names fall out of use, regional and personal variations occur.

The task of indexing names for applique is easier than indexing pieced designs because there are fewer names for applique in print or in the oral tradition. Most pieced designs are from commercial sources—the pattern companies and periodicals that generated the designs after 1890. But most standard applique designs developed decades before the advent of the commercial sources. By the time names were being recorded in print, quiltmakers had lost interest in applique. The fact that fewer names for applique have been published is the major reason you will find many unnamed designs in this index. Today's nameless pattern may have had a mid-nineteenth century name that is now lost because it was never recorded, but my current belief is that the emphasis on pattern names developed after the heyday of the applique quilt.

Even the word "applique"—the standard name in use today—seems to have had little use in the nineteenth century. Applique is derived from a French verb "appliquer," with the same Latin root "applicare" (to attach to) as our English "apply" (to put on). I have never seen the word in a diary or letter, as the word "pieced" occasionally is. "Applique" with or without the accent, has appeared in mid-century published sources. *The Lady's Work Box Companion* and *The Ladies Guide to Embroidery and Applique*, (without the accent), both published in Philadelphia about 1850, contain the earliest American attributions I have found. But because these are American revisions of English pamphlets, the name may have had little currency here.

In 1896, the *Ladies Home Journal* published an "applique daisy patch" (with the accent) but the use is unusual for the time. An unnamed clipping in a scrapbook dating to about 1890 included an applique pattern sent by a reader who had no words to describe it: "This style of patchwork is not so easily made as common patchwork," she wrote. In a 1911 article on appliqued pillow designs by Marie Webster, the *Ladies Home Journal* had a similar problem distinguishing between "the real patchwork method" and "pieced patchwork." The article did not use the word applique but the seamstress "applied" the flowers.[28] It may be that at the time, the old words for the technique had passed out of the vernacular and the more formal or foreign word "applique" had not yet come into common use.

The most commonly used old-fashioned synonym for applique is "laid-work." Variations of the word have roots in the Renaissance Italian term intarsia (inlaid) embroidery. Early-twentieth-century authors often used both old and new terms to make it clear to their readers what they were talking about. During the 1920s, the Ladies Art Company used "applique" but explained that the technique once was called "laid work." *The American Woman* described "laidwork, that is the leaves, stems, 'rose,' etc. are cut from red and green cloth and felled to a square of white cotton." In her 1915 book Webster used "applique" with an accent, but also used "laid" or "laid-on work," among other terms. Such written evidence of that term in the nineteenth century is sparse. A South Carolina fair offered a prize for a "laid work quilt."[29]

There are also different types of applique, distinguished in the past by variations of the term laid work. In 1882, English writers Caulfeild and Saward described inlaid and onlaid applique using the words to discuss applique that is added to a background versus that in which the ground is cut away to reveal other layers.[30] Today we call this last subcategory "reverse applique" and associate it with Panama's San Blas Indians who use it to create molas. The technique was quite common in nineteenth-century American applique quilts, and many of the elements of the patterns indexed in this book could be onlaid or inlaid.

Needlework historian Susan Burrows Swan traces the inlay technique to the eighteenth century. A 1774 Savannah newspaper advertisement offered a reward for the return of a bed quilt with a tree-of-life design, "a large tree (inlaid work) with a peacock at the root and five small birds on the branches."[31] The verbal distinction between inlay and onlay work continues in the cowboy bootmaking trade where most designs are cut out of the boot leg, revealing another color underneath (inlay). The bootmakers also add leather shapes atop (onlay).

Other distinctions in turn-of-the-century quilt terminology include "patched" versus "pieced" for applique and piecework, respectively. Webster in 1915 used "patched quilt" as a synonym for applique. In the late 1920s, Ruby Short McKim told readers of her book on quilt patterns: "There was a difference between the 'piece' quilts and 'patch' quilts. And contrary to what you might expect, the patch variety was the aristocrat and the pieced the poor relation. For 'patch,' sometimes called 'sewed-on' or 'laid work' meant the appliques and required new cloth."[32]

In the literature of the 1930s, writers describing quilts consistently use the word applique as the standard term. By that point, they no longer felt it necessary to explain that "applique" was a synonym for anything. Today's quilters would be confused by patterns for laid work, sewed-on or felled quilts. The old-fashioned terms still linger in the vernacular, however. I recently interviewed Texan Arthur Lambrecht who has been making quilts since 1910, quilts he described to me as "laid work or applique."[33]

The Decline of Applique

Applique quilts fell out of favor towards the end of the last century. Again, changes in fashion, technology and American culture affected the popularity of the technique. Quiltmakers around the country turned to American cottons after the Civil War. As analine dyes created in laboratories came to dominate the market after 1870, cottons became less reliable. Green was especially fugitive, prone to fade to shades of brown, the reason so many red, tan and white applique quilts survive. By 1900 the cottons were unreliable enough that women may have abandoned applique because they could not find fast fabrics in the appropriate shades. Former mill worker Harriet Robinson complained in 1898, "As for cheap American prints, who prefers to buy them nowadays? Certainly no woman who remembers with affection the good, pretty, durable and *washable*...old time calico."[34]

New quilt styles developed as the passion for Turkey red prints was succeeded by crazes for brown calicos, complex shirting prints, and newly inexpensive silks. Brown calico log cabin quilts were a fad in the 1870s and silk crazy quilts the rage of the 1880s.

The sewing machine made its way into American homes during those decades with significant impact on the handwork that applique required. Girls who had received their needlework education after the advent of the machine lacked hand sewing skills and the incentive to practice them. Many of the applique quilts made in the last quarter of the nineteenth century reflect lower standards for handwork. Curves lack grace, patterns lack detail and stitches lack fine technique. Some women used their new machines to fasten their applique work, but only a few could achieve the complexity of hand applique with the machine stitch.

Just as interest in applique waned, the printed pattern began to replace the designs that had passed hand to hand. The national magazines and periodicals created national styles with an emphasis on new and complex pieced patterns. The Ladies Art Company, one of the first companies to offer patchwork patterns in the sheet, showed only 19 appliqued designs out of 400 patterns in their turn-of-the-century catalog, *Diagrams of Quilts, Sofa and Pincushion Patterns*. By that date, taste and technology had combined to make applique an old fashioned and nearly forgotten art in most of the country. One exception was in southern Pennsylvania, where women continued making applique quilts through the first decades of the new century.

Nancy Page Quilt Club---By Florence La Ganke

Beginning of the Magic Vine Quilt.

The Applique Revival

In 1917, *Hearth and Home* magazine announced that "the old-time 'laid-work' or applique patchwork has come in again." After decades of neglect, the quilt-making public showed a renewed fascination with the technique. Taste, however, relegated the classic red and green floral quilts to the attic. Homemakers responded to a different look characterized by new fabrics, patterns and color schemes. Marie Webster, designing for the *Ladies Home Journal*, was a major factor in the change. She first called for a new look in a 1911 article "The New Patchwork Quilts." Her innovations included naturalistic florals, a contrast to the conventionalized roses and tulips of the nineteenth century. She harmonized light colors to match twentieth-century interior design, and based many of her patterns on the medallion format rather than the block repeat. She presented her original designs by taking advantage of technological and style changes in magazine illustrations. Colored pictures specified the desired shades and new page designs pictured the whole quilt as a rectangular composition, minimizing the earlier emphasis on a single block and maximizing the importance of border and edge.

By the 1920s applique was again a fad. The 1922 version of the catalog from the Ladies Art Catalog had a new name, *Quilt Patterns: Pieced and Appliqued*, and a new section on "attractive applique designs with borders." Quilters obtained traditional patterns from such commercial sources, rather than from friends or family. One popular source for literal copies of antique quilts was Carlie Sexton, who wrote for *Better Homes and Gardens* and ran an Illinois pattern business.

A few companies followed Marie Webster's lead with modern designs. The St. Louis Fancy Work Company was an innovator in the teens with graceful designs inspired by art nouveau. In the early 1920s quilters who wanted something new looked to *Needlecraft Magazine*. As the 1920s ended many more designers responded to the modern look. One widely syndicated artist was Florence La Ganke Harris, who wrote a column under the name Nancy Page. Although her pieced patterns were traditional, her appliqued designs were modern versions of the old applique sampler, each series a variation on a theme such as children's toys or the zodiac. (See Series patterns numbered in the 70s.)

Loretta Leitner Rising wrote a daily column for the *Chicago Tribune* from 1933 though the 1940s, using the name Nancy Cabot. She revived traditional applique patterns but also invented numerous designs in the 2000 patterns she published, which also appeared under different pen names in the *Progressive Farmer*, the *New York Daily News* and other periodicals. Nancy Cabot patterns are the largest source of twentieth-century applique, (note how many designs she originated in the patterns numbered 34 and 35). Despite her amazing production, she was not so influential as less prolific designers like Webster and Page. Far more quilts survive in their designs than in Cabot's quirky blocks.

In the index I have indicated patterns I believe to have been designed by twentieth-century artists with a "D"; traditional nineteenth-century designs are marked with a "T". My list of criteria for categorizing a pattern as "D" is short and rather subjective. The first is that I have not seen any evidence of the design in nineteenth-century quilts. The second is merely that it *looks* like a twentieth-century design. Certain design characteristics do give a look to twentieth-century applique. The new color schemes made possible by improved aniline dyes are notable on the quilts if not the patterns. Pinks, lavenders and shades of tangerine replaced the Turkey red cottons and indigo blues. Distinctive light greens with a bluish-gray cast replaced the dark greens so prone to fading. Although most patterns were printed in black and white, the designers often suggested color. Nancy Cabot communicates the fashionable look effectively in her 1933 description of an 1840 pattern. "In the early days of its history only strong colors were available, and, like other old patterns of its time, it was executed in bright reds and greens. A twentieth-century quiltmaker would undoubtedly prefer dainty pastel shades."[35] Marie Webster included actual fabric swatches in her mail-order patterns to assist the customer with color selection.

The change in color schemes was related to trends in home-decorating during the 1920s. For years the kitchens, bathrooms and bedding of the well-to-do had been white, the color of cleanliness. But modern decorating dictated pastel, color-coordinated kitchens and bathrooms, a compromise between color and hospital standards for sanitation since pastels showed the dirt as well as white did.[36] When white was the fashion, magazines recommended white bed-spreads rather than "unsightly" and "unhealthy" patched quilts,[37] but as light colors became fashionable, light-colored quilts became the bedding recommended by the home improvement experts.

Modern quilts were more than a new color scheme, however. Symmetries moved away from the formal, four-way mirror image or the bouquet of three blooms. Flowers undulated across the block echoing art nouveau naturalism. Blocks often featured a single flower rather than a symmetrical bouquet. Medallion arrangements were constructed with concentric borders of graceful florals.

The eight-lobed rosette no longer dominated, although florals remained the primary subject matter. A wider variety of species was depicted; pansies, poppies and iris were especially popular. Roses remained important, but like other flowers, they were appliqued with naturalistic shape and shading. Many of the conventionalized florals had four, five or six petals, motifs that had been popular in European embroidery and other decorative arts for centuries but that had played little part in American applique between 1840 and 1920. Pictorial designs went beyond florals. Sunbonnet Sue and her grown-up counterpart, the Colonial Lady, were fashionable as were butterflies, cuddly animals, and nursery rhyme characters.

Although the new applique designs were numerous in publications after 1915, pieced patterns continued to dominate the commercial pattern network. The syndicated column that appeared under the names Laura Wheeler and Alice Brooks, for example, included only four applique designs among 90 patterns in their newspaper advertising in the 1930s.[38] Ruby McKim's *101 Quilt Patterns*, published in 1931, contained 11 patterns with applique work. Only a few companies like Boag, Rainbow and Webster's Practical Patchwork, specialized in applique or embroidery over pieced patterns. Applique was the mainstay of the quilt kit industry, a facet of the pattern business that expanded from 1920 to 1960. Paragon, Rainbow and Bucilla each sold their own versions of elaborate floral medallion kits. Today, a few kits continue to be available to quiltmakers who are more interested in a beautiful bedspread than originality.

During the 1950s and 1960s, as interest in quiltmaking faded in cities and patterns disappeared from periodicals, quilters who did any applique work relied on kits. Few designers generated new patterns; one exception was the Laura Wheeler/Alice Brooks syndicate. Their artists continued to produce simple patterns for kittens, puppies, flowers and cowboys through the lean years of quiltmaking.

Recent Interest in Applique

Although piecework was the early focus of the 1970s quilt revival, innovative applique designs by women such as Jean Ray Laury, Virginia Avery and Chris Wolf Edmonds influenced many to create original pattern and pictorial applique. In the late 1980s a flurry of collecting interest in Baltimore Album quilts inspired seamstresses to look back to the mid-nineteenth century for inspiration. Elly Sienkeiwicz's series of Baltimore pattern books and Jeana Kimball's designs for traditional applique have given quiltmakers new access to complex blocks. Jeanne Benson and others design new blocks for the 1990s.[39] As applique again comes into its own, we will see quiltmakers at the turn of the twenty-first century creating quilts to equal the masterpieces of the 1840s and 1930s.

Footnotes

1 Marie Webster, *Quilts: Their Story and How To Make Them* (New York: Doubleday, Page and Co., 1915). Schuppe Von Gwinner, *The History of the Patchwork Quilt* (West Chester, PA: Schiffer, 1988). John Michael Vlach, *The Afro-American Tradition in the Decorative Arts* (Cleveland: The Cleveland Museum of Art, 1978) 44-54.

2 Von Gwinner, 57-63.

3 Jinny Beyer, *The Art and Technique of Creating Medallion Quilts* (McLean, VA: EPM, 1982).

4 Susan Burrows Swan, *Plain and Fancy: American Women and Their Needlework, 1700-1850* (New York: Holt, Rinehart and Winston, 1977); Sophia Frances Anne Caulfeild and Blanche C. Saward, *The Dictionary of Needlework* (London: L.Upton Gill, 1882) 10.

5 Georgiana Brown Harbeson, *American Needlework* (New York: Bonanaza Books, 1938) 136.

6 *The Lady's Work Box Companion* (Philadelphia: J. & J.L. Gihon, undated) 26; *The Lady's Guide to Embroidery and Applique* Philadelphia: W.A. Leary, undated. ca. 1850)

7 Viriginia Gunn, "Template Quilt Construction and Its Offshoots: From Godey's Lady's Book to Mountain Mist," in Jeannette Lasansky (ed.) *Pieced By Mother: Symposium Papers* (Lewisburg, PA: Oral Traditions Project: 1988) 69-72.

8 Jack Larkin, *The Reshaping of Everyday Life 1790-1840* (New York: Harper and Row, 1988) 146.

9 Letter from Elizabeth Hodgdon, quoted in Thomas Dublin, *Farm to Factory: Women's Letters 1830-1860* (New York: Columbia University Press, 1981) 55-57.

10 Jeannette Lasansky, *A Good Start: The Aussteier or Dowry* (Lewisburg, PA: Oral Traditions Project, 1990) 43.

11 Reinhard Peesch, *The Ornament in European Folk Art*, transl. Ruth Michaeilis-Jena and Patrick Murray (New York: Alpine Fine Arts Collection, 1982).

12 I am grateful to Nancy Hornback for calling my attention to Peesch's work and the similarities between American quilt design and German folk art. Nancy Hornback, *Quilts in Red and Green: The Flowering of Folk Design in 19th Century America* (Wichita: Wichita-Sedgwick County Historical Museum, 1992).

13 Wilbur Zelinsky, *The Cultural Geography of the United States* (Englewood Cliffs, NJ: Prentice Hall, 1973).

14 Hornback, 3.

15 Phoebe George Bradford, "The Diaries of Phoebe George Bradford," Wilson W. Emerson (ed.), *Delaware History*, 16, 1974.

16 Davida Tenenbaum Deutsch, "Needlework Patterns and Their Use in America," *The Magazine Antiques*, Vol. CXXXIX, No. 2, February, 1991, 368-381.

17 Philadelphia Museum of Art, *Pennsylvania German Art 1683-1850* (Chicago: University of Chicago Press, 1984) 307.

18 Deutsch.

19 Levina B. Urbino, and Henry Day, *Art Recreations* (Boston: J.E. Tilton and Co., 1860) 145.

20 Vicki McIntyre. "Theorem Paintings," *Early American Life*, August 1981, 28.

21 Diana Church, "The Baylis Stenciled Quilt," *Uncoverings 1983* (Mill Valley, CA: American Quilt Study Group, 1984) 75.

22 *Godey's Lady's Book*, January, 1830. 13, quoted in Margaret Vincent, *The Ladies Work Table: Domestic Needlework in Nineteenth Century America* (Allentown, PA: Allentown Art Museum, 1988).

23 *Arts Companion, or a New Assistant for the Ingenious in Three Parts* (London and Dublin, 1749), quoted in Deutsch, 376.

24 Wilene Smith, "Quilt Blocks—Or—Quilt Patterns," *Uncoverings 1986* (Mill Valley, CA: American Quilt Study Group, 1987).

25 Emily Hawley Gillespie, *A Secret To Be Buried: The Diary of Emily Hawley Gillespie, 1858-1888*, Judy Nolte Lensink (ed.) (Iowa City: University of Iowa Press, 1989) 43.

26 Diaries of Elizabeth Porter Phelps, Pamela Brown and Chastina Rix, quoted in Lynn Bonfield, "Diaries of New England Quilters Before 1860," *Uncoverings*, (San Francisco: American Quilt Study Group, Volume 9, 1989)189, 192.

27 Letter from Elizabeth Nessly Myer, March, 24, 1860, quoted in Kay Atwood, *Mill Creek Journal* (Ashland, OR: By the author, 1987) 120; Quilt # 10.398, Shelburne Museum, Shelburne, VT; Karoline Patterson Bresenhan and Nancy O'Bryant Puentes, *Lone Stars: A Legacy of Texas Quilts, 1836-1936* (Austin, TX: University of Texas Press, 1986) 40; Bets Ramsey and Merikay Waldvogel, *The Quilts of Tennessee: Images of Domestic Life Prior to 1930* (Nashville, TN: Rutledge Hill, 1986) 9.

28 Jane Benson. "Designs for Patchwork Quilts," *Ladies Home Journal*, November, 1896. 24; Marie Webster, *Ladies Home Journal*, 1911.

29 Catalog of Quilts and Quilting, (St. Louis: Ladies Art Company, undated)1; *The American Woman*, undated clipping; Webster, *Quilts*; Virginia Gunn, "Quilts At Ohio Fairs," *Uncoverings* (San Francisco: American Quilt Study Group, Volume 9, 1989) 126.

30 Caulfeild and Saward, 8.

31 Swan, 228.

32 Webster, 94. Ruby Short McKim, *101 Quilt Patterns*, (Independence, MO: McKim Studios, 1931) 16.

33 Telephone interview with Arthur Lambrecht, November 18, 1991.

34 Harriet H. Robinson, *Loom and Spindle or Life Among the Early Mill Girls.* (New York: Thos. Y. Crowell and Co., 1898) 212.

35 Nancy Cabot, "Rose of 1840," *Chicago Tribune*, July 16, 1933.

36 Harvey Green, *The Uncertainty of Everyday Life 1815-1945*, (New York: Harper Collins, 1992) 184-5.

37 "Bed-Clothes," *Arthur's Home Magazine*. October, 1883, 63.

38 Merikay Waldvogel, "Anne Orr's Quilts," *Uncoverings* (San Francisco: American Quilt Study Group, Volume 11, 1991) 21.

39 Elly Sienkiewicz's books include *Spoken Without a Word* (Washington D.C.: By the Author,1983) and *Baltimore Beauties and Beyond, Volumes 1 and 2* (Lafayette, CA: C&T). Jeanna Kimball's include *Reflections of Baltimore and Red and Green, An Applique Tradition* (Bothell, WA: That Patchwork Place, 1989 & 1990). Jeanne Benson, *The Art and Technique of Applique* (McLean, VA: E.P.M., 1991).

Quilt by Christina Hays Malcolm (ca. 1820–1880), dated 1873. Collection: Helen F. Spencer Museum of Art, University of Kansas. Gift of Ira James. These elaborate versions of the feathered wheel are numbered 15.5 and usually called **Princess Feather.**

PART 2

How to Use the Index

The patterns are indexed by design rather than name, so that you can find an unnamed pattern. The "Key to Major Categories," which follows, will direct you to a specific area where another key will help you find the page with your pattern. Applique's diversity dictates a different approach to classification from that used for pieced designs. Rather than looking for an exact match to an unknown applique pattern, you must try to fit it into a class of designs.

I have grouped the designs into numerous classes, generally based on the designs' geometry. Many of the nineteenth century patterns, for example, are symmetrical with a four-way, mirror-image balance. (If a cross were drawn north to south and east to west across the design the four corners would be identical.) I begin the index with these symmetrical patterns which are further classified into the following general categories: wreaths (WREATHS), repeats of four elements radiating from the center (FOUR ELEMENTS), repeats of eight identical elements radiating from the center (EIGHT ELEMENTS), eight repeats with four of one element and four of another alternating around a center (FOUR PLUS FOUR ELEMENTS), repeats with nothing in the center (CORNER DESIGNS) and repeats of MORE THAN EIGHT ELEMENTS.

Patterns with different symmetries follow. Basket designs, for example, usually have a two-way mirror image symmetry (only a single line divides them into equal halves). They are classified as CONTAINERS under OTHER SYMMETRIES. Animals, which are usually shown in profile, have no symmetry in the quilt block. You cannot draw a line and find a mirror-image of the design. These are also classified as OTHER SYMMETRIES towards the end of that category. There are numerous categories and sub-categories in this OTHER SYMMETRY section; most of them are pictorial and rather easy to find.

There are some twentieth-century blocks that were designed to be arranged as a series, a group of similar designs with a theme. These are classified as SERIES, followed by MEDALLIONS which have a central design focus often surrounded by a series of borders. There is also a small category of STRIPS, in which the design is set together in linear fashion, rather than as blocks. Last is a small category of SASH AND BLOCK DESIGNS, blocks which require a certain patchwork sashing to make the pattern.

Each of the patterns is numbered with a decimal system. The basic numbers range from 1 to 100 followed by a decimal point. (Numbers beyond 100 have been assigned to pieced patterns in my previously published *Encyclopedia of Pieced Quilt Patterns*). If you plan to use a computer with this numbering system please read the note at the end of this section concerning a computerized numbering system.

Some of the patterns can be pieced or are partially pieced and appliqued. If I indexed them in the *Encyclopedia of Pieced Quilt Patterns* I give a numeric cross reference. I also cross reference patterns within the *Encyclopedia of Applique*.

The letters "T" or "D" accompany each pattern. "T" means the design is, in my opinion, a traditional nineteenth-century pattern; "D" means it is likely a design that originated in a twentieth-century designer's studio. Occasionally a pattern's origins are not obvious, and I have left a blank.

The pattern names are followed by a source (in some cases I had only a clipping with no source and in other cases—I confess—I forgot to write it down). The source is either a quilt of that pattern or a published source for the name and design. To find out more about the published source, read the references that follow the numerical index.

When several sources give the same name for a pattern I give you only the earliest source. For example, if the Ladies Art Company's catalog and Marguerite Ickis give the same name for a design I give the Ladies Art Company as the source since their 19th century catalog predates Ickis's 1949 book. When several sources have published the same design with different names I have listed them in chronological order. The first name for each design is the oldest name I could find in print.

An alphabetical cross reference at the end of the book can help you find the pattern if you know the name. It also gives you lists of patterns named for specific themes, such as iris, oak leaves or Kansas.

A Note for Computer Users

The patterns are indexed with a two digit number plus up to three decimal places. When you are setting up a file for these numbers be sure to make room for two digits and three decimal places. However, you might want to coordinate this file with my *Encyclopedia of Pieced Quilt Patterns* (Paducah, KY: American Quilter's Society, 1993) which uses the numbers from 111 to 9999. You must then create space for four digits before the decimal and three after. You must also enter all numbers as seven digits. Thus a wreath numbered 1.31 in the *Encyclopedia of Applique* should be entered as 0001.310.

One use for my numerical indexes is to communicate about pattern by number. I wish I could say that every applique design now has an "official" number, but this is not the case. Applique is too spontaneous to become official. My intent is to create a system for numbering that also applies to unknown patterns. The number before the decimal point is unique to a specific category. Overall Boys, for example, are numbered 48 with individual designs having different decimal numbers. If you find an Overall Boy that is unlisted you can do one of two things: 1) You can give the pattern a decimal number that I haven't used. Start with 48 and give it one of the 1000 possible decimal numbers. I have used up only sixteen. 2) Your other option is to call all unknown Overall Boys 48.000.

Key to Major Categories

Go through the descriptions below in order beginning with # 1.

1.
— The design is organized in blocks. Go to 2 below.

— The design is organized into strips. See Strips, patterns numbered 90.

— The design is organized around a central image. See Medallions, patterns numbered 80. Check the outline for subcategories.

2.
— The blocks are identical. Go to 3 below.

— The blocks are a series (a twentieth-century designer pattern with each block a variation of a theme). See Series, patterns numbered 70. Check the outline for subcategories.

— The blocks are a sampler of different patterns. Each block will have to be identified separately. Go to 3 below.

3.
— The block is a full wreath. See Wreaths, patterns numbered 1-4. Check the outline for subcategories.

— The block is an open wreath. See Leaves and Open Wreaths, patterns numbered 43.

— The block is not a wreath. Go to 4 below.

4.
— The block design is a 4-way symmetrical repeat (if folded in quarters, the quarters are essentially identical). Go to 5 below.

— The block design is asymmetrical or has two-way symmetry (if folded in half, the halves are essentially identical). Go to 7 below.

5.
— The symmetrical pattern radiates from a central design. Go to 6 below.

— The symmetrical pattern is empty in the center. See Corner Designs, patterns numbered 26.

6.
— The central design has four identical radiating motifs. See Four Elements, patterns numbered 5-13. Check the outline for subcategories.

— The central design has eight identical radiating motifs. See Eight Elements, patterns numbered 14-15. Check the outline for subcategories.

— The central design has eight radiating motifs, four of one motif, four of another. See Four Plus Four Arms patterns nmbered 16-25. Check the outline for subcategories.

— The central design has more than eight radiating motifs. See More Than Eight Elements, patterns numbered 27.

7.

— Go through the list below and choose the first description that applies to your pattern:

— The design is based on a repeat of five elements or has flowers with five petals. See Five Elements, patterns numbered 34-35.

— The design is based on a repeat of six radiating motifs or has flowers with six petals. See Six Petals, patterns number 36.

— The design has seven radiating motifs. See Seven Elements, patterns numbered 36.9.

— The design is a floral bouquet in a basket, pot, bowl, etc. See Containers, numbered 38-42. Check the outline for subcategories.

— The design is a floral bouquet without a container. See Bouquets, patterns numbered 28-37. Check the outline for subcategories.

— The design is a leaf. See Leaves and Open Wreaths, patterns numbered 43.

— The design is an open wreath. See Leaves and Open Wreaths, patterns numbered 43.

— The design is a floral tree. See Floral Trees, patterns numbered 44.

— The design is a fruit or vegetable. See Fruits and Vegetables, patterns numbered 46.

— The design does not have four-way symmetry and is not in the above categories. See Other Symmetries-Miscellaneous, patterns numbered 45.

— The picture represents a person. See Human Figures, patterns numbered 47-50. Check the outline for subcategories.

— The picture is an animal, insect, object or symbol. See patterns numbered 51-60. Check the outline for subcategories.

The Numbering System in Outline

Four-Way Symmetry 1-27

Wreaths 1-4

Leaves, Fruit and Miscellaneous   1

Floral   2-4

Four Elements 5-13

Four Leaves   5

Four Fleur-de-Lis   6

Four Buds   7

Four Tulips   8

Four Flowers, Fruit and Miscellaneous   9

Four Hearts   9.8

Four Miscellaneous Elements   9.9

Floral Centers. Four Elements   10-13

Eight Elements 14-15

Miscellaneous   14

Princess Feathers   15

Four Plus Four Elements 16-25

Fruit   16

Reels   17

Combs   18

Miscellaneous   19-25

The Index to Traditional and Modern Applique Patterns

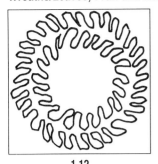

1.12
T* Unnamed—
Finley

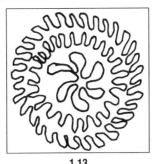

1.13
T Feather Crown—
Finley
T Feather Crown with a Ragged Robin
Center—
Hall and Kretsinger

1.21
Wreath of Leaves—
Boag kit

1.22
T Unnamed—
from an album dated 1857

1.26
T Foliage Wreath—
Ickis, pg. 61

1.27
T Wreath of Strawberry Leaves—
Sienkiewicz

1.28
T Unnamed—
from an album in Finley

1.31
D* Rose Garland—
Nancy Cabot, *Chicago Tribune* 1947

1.33
T Wreath of Cherries—
Comfort

1.34
T Cherry Wreaths—
from a quilt ca. 1860 in Orlofsky,
fig. 70

1.35
T Wreath of Cherries—
Sienkiewicz

1.37
D* Primrose—
Aunt Martha Studios
Bridal Wreath—
Herrschners kit

1.4
T Bachelor's Dream—Irwin
Vase of Roses and
Cherries—Bresenhan/Texas
Quilts of Tennessee found several
examples in Tennessee

1.51
T Wreath of Grapes—
Ickis

1.55
Holly Wreath—
Nancy Cabot, *Chicago Tribune*

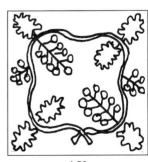

1.56
Muscatel Grape—
Boag kit

* **T** = Traditional nineteenth-century pattern   * **D** = Twentieth-century design studio pattern

1.57
T Grapes—
Nancy Cabot, *Chicago Tribune* 1935

1.62
D Rose Garland—
Nancy Cabot, *Chicago Tribune* 1947

1.64
D Garland of Leaves—
Nancy Cabot, *Chicago Tribune* 1933

1.65
D Bridal Wreath—
Ickis, pg. 118

1.67
D Brenda's Rosebud Wreath—
Sienkiewicz

1.69
D Pilot's Wheel—
Rural New Yorker

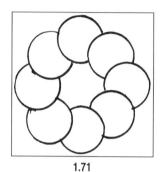

1.71
D Unnamed—
Wheeler/Brooks

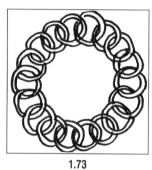

1.73
T Unnamed—
From an album dated 1848

Wreaths/Floral 2-4

1.76
T Unnamed—
alternates with a Democrat Rose in
Whitehill quilt at Denver Art Museum

2.13
T Grape Wreath—
name inscribed on quilt ca. 1870
Shelburne #10.323

2.16
T Wreath of Roses—
name inscribed on quilt ca. 1870
Shelburne #10.323

2.18
D Sweet Pea Wreath—
Nancy Cabot, *Chicago Tribune*

2.23
T Rose Wreath—
Ladies Art Company #262

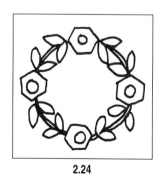

2.24
T Flower Wreath—
Grandmother Clark Book 23

2.31
T Conventional Rose Wreath—Webster
Wreath of Roses—Webster
Rose Wreath—Aunt Martha Studios
Kentucky Rose—Finley

2.32
T The Garden Wreath—
Finley

2.33
T North Carolina Rose—
Aunt Martha 1933

2.34
T Dahlia Wreath—
Hall and Kretsinger pg. 171

2.36
T Wreath of Roses—
Ladies Art Company #189

2.4
T Wreath of Roses—
Carlie Sexton

2.51
D Cluster of Roses—
Webster ca. 1925

2.53
D Hollyhock Wreath—
McKim ca. 1930 & Nancy Cabot,
Chicago Tribune 1933

2.55
T Wreath of Roses—
The Family 1913

2.57
T Wreath of Roses—
Rural New Yorker (note wreath is
not a circle)

2.61
T Wreath of Roses—
Ickis

2.62
T Wreath of Roses—
Hall and Kretsinger
Garden Wreath—
Hall and Kretsinger

2.63
T Kentucky Rose—
St. Louis Fancywork, Hall and
Kretsinger

2.64
T Rose of Heaven—
Nancy Cabot, *Chicago Tribune* 1934

2.65
T President's Wreath—
Hall and Kretsinger

2.66
T Martha Washington Wreath—
Rural New Yorker

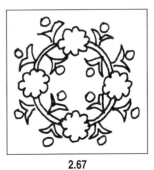

2.67
T Roses & Bells—
Nancy Cabot, *Chicago Tribune* 1935

2.68
T Unnamed—
Modern Priscilla, March, 1926

2.69
T Newark Wreath—
Nancy Cabot, *Chicago Tribune*

2.71
T The Rose Quilt—
Ladies Home Journal 1908

2.72
T President's Wreath—
Grandmother Clark

2.73
T Centennial Wreath—
Nancy Cabot, *Chicago Tribune* 1938

2.74
T Indian Paintbrush—
Finley

2.75
T Wreath of Roses—
Hearth and Home

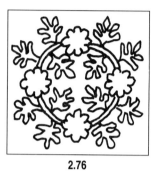

2.76
T President's Wreath—
Finley, plate 27

2.77
T Bud and Rose Wreath—
Ickis, pg. 138

2.78
T Wild Rose Wreath—
Ickis, pg. 66

3.1
D Wreath—
Nancy Cabot, *Chicago Tribune* 1936

3.2
D Moonflower—
Nancy Cabot, *Chicago Tribune* 1934

3.31
T Dahlia Wreath—
Nancy Cabot, *Chicago Tribune* 1933

3.32
T Wreath of Carnations—
Hall and Kretsinger, pg. 124

3.33
T Wreath of Roses—
The Family 1913

3.34
T Dahlia Wreath—
name inscribed on a quilt ca. 1870
Shelburne #10.323

3.5
T Rose and Bud Wreath—
Ladies Art Company #6064
Rose Wreath—
Nancy Cabot, *Chicago Tribune*

3.36
T Wreath of Roses—
Hall and Kretsinger, pg. 149

3.37
T Unnamed—
from an album dated 1850

3.42
T Rose Wreath—
Nancy Cabot, *Chicago Tribune*

3.43
T Unnamed—
Prudence Penny

3.48
T Unnamed—
Clark/Ohio

3.5
T Wreath of Wild Roses—
Hall and Kretsinger

3.63
T Iowa Rose—
Carlie Sexton

3.64
T Wreath of Pansies—
Hall and Kretsinger pg. 184
(mislabeled; should have read Iowa
Rose Wreath)

3.7
T Iowa Rose—
Nancy Cabot, *Chicago Tribune* 1933
D Des Moines Rose—
Nancy Cabot, *Chicago Tribune* 1937

3.83
T Unnamed—
from an album dated 1851

3.84
T Fleur-de-lis with Folded Rose
Buds—
Sienkiewicz

3.92
D Tulip Circle—
Wheeler/Brooks

3.94
D Crocus Wreath—
Nancy Cabot, *Chicago Tribune* 1933

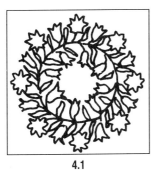

4.1
T Hawaiian Flower—
Nancy Cabot, *Chicago Tribune* 1935

4.21
D Tulip Time—
Hinson/Quilting Manual

4.25
T Strawberry Wreath—
name inscribed on quilt ca. 1870
Shelburne #10.323

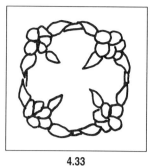

4.33
D Pansy Design—
Ladies Art Company #6065
Iowa Rose Wreath—Hall and Kretsinger.
Probably mislabeled; should have read
Wreath of Pansies.

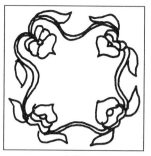

4.35
D Pansy—
Mrs. Danner

4.4
D Wild Rose Wreath—
Ladies Home Journal 8/1911

4.53
D Wreath of Morning Glories—
Comfort

4.55
D Morning Glory—
The Family 1913

4.6
Unnamed—
Clark/Ohio

4.72
T Victorian Rose—
quilt by Whitehill Denver Art
Museum

4.78
D Wreath of Roses—
Webster ca. 1925

4.81
T Unnamed—
from an album dated 1854

4.82
D Primrose Wreath—
Webster design ca. 1925

4.84
D Nasturtium Wreath—
Webster design ca. 1925

4.86
D Unnamed—
Aunt Martha/*Prize-Winning Quilts*
ca. 1933

4.87
D Lily Design—
Comfort

4.92
D Flower Wreath—
Nancy Cabot, *Chicago Tribune* 1934

4.94
D Wild Rose Wreath—
Rural New Yorker 1934

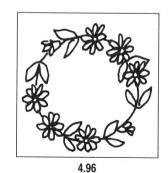

4.96
D Wreath of Daisies—
Nancy Cabot, *Chicago Tribune* 1933

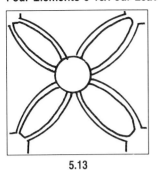

5.13
T Job's Tears—
Nancy Cabot, *Chicago Tribune*
1933. See as a pieced pattern
#3079

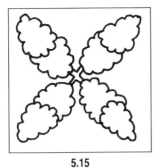

5.15
D Red Hot Poker—
Nancy Cabot, *Chicago Tribune* 1934
Pompom—
Nancy Cabot, *Chicago Tribune* 1937

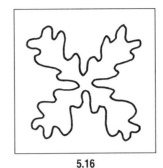

5.16
T Tobacco Leaf—
Nancy Cabot, *Chicago Tribune* 1933

5.17
T Unnamed—
from an album dated 1857. A
similar leaf alternated with a Double
Irish Chain block called Double Irish
Cross in *Country Life* 1923

5.18
D Block from the Leaf Quilt—
Nancy Page. See #71.5

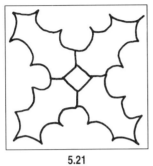

5.21
D Oak Leaves—
Nancy Cabot, *Chicago Tribune* 1937

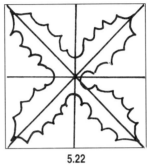

5.22
D Holly Leaves—
Nancy Cabot, *Chicago Tribune* 1936

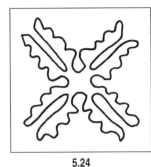

5.24
T Tobacco Leaves—
Finley plate 59

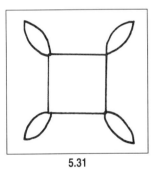

5.31
T Unnamed—
from a quilt ca. 1840

5.32
T Unnamed—
from a quilt ca. 1840

5.33
T Honey Bee—
Nancy Cabot, *Chicago Tribune* 1933
T Birds in the Air—
Coats and Clark 1942. See as
pieced patterns #2217-2218.

5.34
T Antique Fleur-de-lis—
Nancy Cabot, *Chicago Tribune* 1934

5.36
T Turkey Tracks—
Finley. See as a pieced pattern
#3109.
Wandering Foot—
Finley

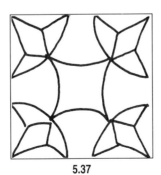

5.37
T The Swallow—
Rural New Yorker 1937
Burr and Thistle—
Rural New Yorker 1937. See pieced
patterns #3096-3109.

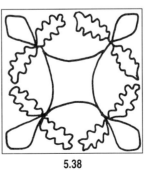

5.38
T Aunt Dinah's Delight—
Carlie Sexton

5.39
T Aunt Dinah's Delight—
Nancy Cabot, *Chicago Tribune*

55

5.42
T Conventional Tulip—
Farmer's Wife 10/1929

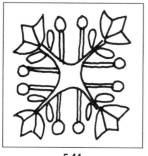

5.44
T Unnamed—
from a quilt in MacDowell/Michigan
pg. 53

5.45
T Unnamed—
from an album dated 1853

5.47
T Rose Leaf—
Rural New Yorker

5.49
T Amazon Lily—
Nancy Cabot, *Chicago Tribune* 1937

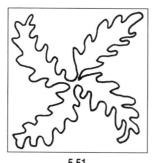

5.51
T Unnamed—
from an album dated 1847

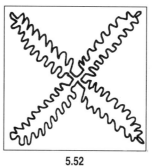

5.52
T Princess Feather—
Bresenhan/Texas

5.54
T Unnamed—
from an album dated 1844

5.55
T Laurel Leaves—
Shelburne Museum pg. 61

5.62
D Sumach Leaf—
block from the Leaf Quilt by Nancy
Page. See 71.5

5.63
T Unnamed—
from an album dated 1847

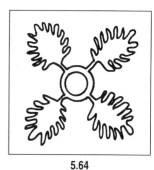

5.64
T Unnamed—
from an album dated 1851

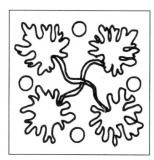

5.66
T Unnamed—
from an album dated 1856

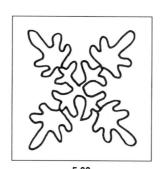

5.68
T Unnamed—
from an album dated 1855

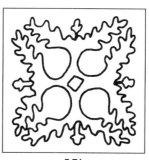

5.71
T Charter Oak—
Finley pg. 124

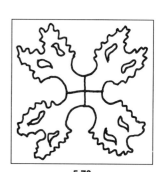

5.72
T Oak Leaf—
Farmer's Wife 1932

Four Leaves 5

5.73
T Maple Leaf—
Ladies Art Company

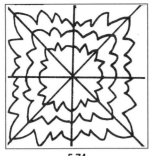

5.74
D Flame Block—
Nancy Cabot, *Chicago Tribune*
Flames—
Nancy Cabot, *Chicago Tribune* 1935

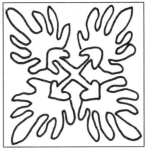

5.76
T Cotton Boll—
from a repeat block quilt, ca. 1860, in
Roberson/North Carolina
T Chrysanthemum—same source

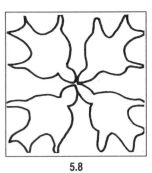

5.8
T Four Little Birds—
Ladies Art Company #303

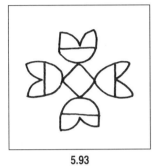

5.93
D Arrowroot Block—
Nancy Cabot, *Chicago Tribune* 1935

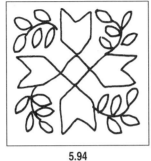

5.94
D Tulip Square—
Nancy Cabot, *Chicago Tribune* 1936

Four Fleur-de-lis 6

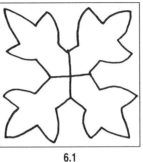

6.1
T Poplar Leaf—
Ladies Art Company #111

6.2
T Philadelphia Beauty—
Ladies Art Company #116

6.3
T Four Frogs—
Ladies Art Company #283

6.4
T Washington Square—
Farm Journal 1/1934

6.5
T Bride's Fancy—
Hearth and Home
Winchester—
Hearth and Home

6.6
T Fleur de Lis—
McKim

Four Buds 7

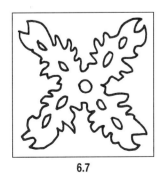

6.7
T Lobster—
Hinson/*Quilting Manual* plate 22

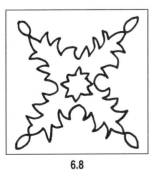

6.8
D Friendship Plume—
Mountain Mist

7.2
T Orange Block—
Nancy Cabot, *Chicago Tribune* 1938

7.4
D Baby Rose—
Carlie Sexton

Four Buds 7　　　　**Four Tulips 8**

7.6
D　Moon Blossoms—
Nancy Cabot, *Chicago Tribune* 1935

8.12
T　Lily of the Valley—
Nancy Cabot, *Chicago Tribune* 1934

8.14
T　Unnamed—
from a clipping ca. 1890

8.16
T　Four Tulips—
Ladies Art Company #453

8.18
T　Lily of the Valley—
Ladies Art Company #391

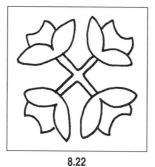

8.22
T　Tulip Tree Leaves—
Hall and Kretsinger

8.24
T　Tulip Tree Leaves—
Webster

8.33
T　Dutch Tulip—
Nancy Cabot, *Chicago Tribune* 1933

8.38
T　Tulip—
from a quilt ca. 1885, in
Roberson/North Carolina, pg. 72

8.43
T　Four Tulips—
Hall and Kretsinger, pg. 122

8.47
D　Lombardy Lily—
Nancy Cabot, *Chicago Tribune* 1938

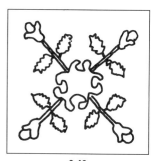

8.49
T　Unnamed—
from a quilt in Lasansky/Pieced,
plate 49

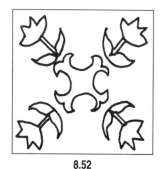

8.52
T　Summer Tulips—
Nancy Cabot, *Chicago Tribune* 1937

8.54
T　Tennessee Tulip—
McKim, *Patchwork Parade of States*

8.56
T　Conventional Tulips—
Rural New Yorker
Gay Tulips—
Needlecraft Magazine 1936

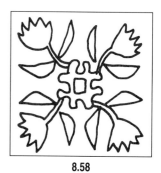

8.58
T　Colonial Patchwork—
Hearth and Home February, 1917

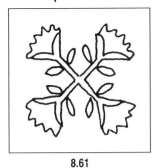

8.61
T Lotus Flower—
Hall and Kretsinger, pg 120

8.63
T Unnamed—
from a quilt, *Quilt Engagement
Calendar* 1977, plate 18

8.64
T Tulip—
from a quilt ca. 1935,
Roberson/North Carolina, pg. 76

8.65
T Tulip Crib Quilt—
Ickis, pg. 102

8.66
T Loretta's Rose—
Hall and Kretsinger, pg. 116

8.67
T Tulip—
Ladies Art Company #449

8.68
T Unnamed—
Aunt Martha, *Prize-Winning Quilts*

8.71
T Lotus Bud—
Hall and Kretsinger

8.73
T Indiana Rose—
Carlie Sexton

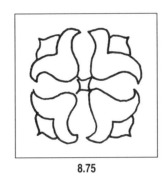

8.75
T Amaryllis—
Nancy Cabot, *Chicago Tribune* 1934
Scarlet Amaryllis—
Nancy Cabot, *Chicago Tribune* 1938

8.83
D Peony—
Ladies Art Company #6073

8.87
D Harebells—
Nancy Cabot, *Chicago Tribune* 1934

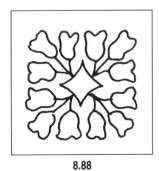

8.88
D St. Peter's Penny—
Nancy Cabot, *Chicago Tribune* 1934

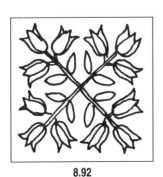

8.92
T Golden Bells—
Nancy Cabot, *Chicago Tribune* 1936

8.94
T $200,000 Tulip—
Sienkeiwicz

8.95
T Unnamed—
from an album dated 1847

9.1
D Good Luck Clover—
Nancy Cabot, *Chicago Tribune* 1934

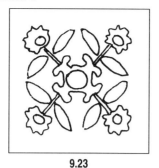

9.23
T Unnamed—
from an album dated 1854

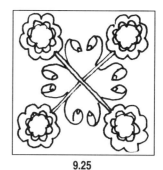

9.25
T Single Stem Rose Variation—
from a quilt ca. 1850,
Kimball pg. 146

9.26
T Original Rose—
Webster plate 51

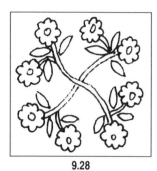

9.28
T Unnamed—
from a quilt, *Quilt Engagement
Calendar* 1980, plate 56

9.32
T Grandmother's Dream—
Carlie Sexton, *Old Fashioned Quilts*
pg. 21

9.34
T Piney—
Carlie Sexton

9.36
D Poinsettia—
Kansas City Star 1931

9.38
T Unnamed—
from an album dated 1852

9.41
D Curling Leaves—
Nancy Cabot, *Chicago Tribune* 1936

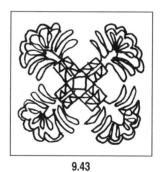

9.43
T Coxcomb—
from a quilt, ca.
1860, Clarke/*Kentucky* pg. 23

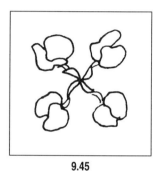

9.45
D Sweet Peas—
Mountain Mist

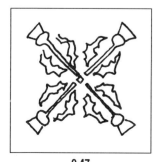

9.47
T Thistle Block—
Nancy Cabot, *Chicago Tribune* 1937

9.48
T Thistles—
Peto, *American Quilts*, pg. 63

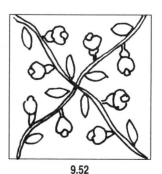

9.52
D Magnolia Buds in Floral Maze—
Baroness Pignatoni in the
Minneapolis Morning Tribune

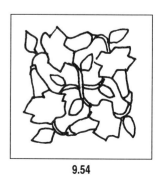

9.54
D Trumpet Vine Block—
Nancy Cabot, *Chicago Tribune*

Four Flowers, Fruits and Miscellaneous 9

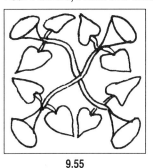

9.55
D Morning Glory—
Nancy Cabot, *Chicago Tribune* 1937

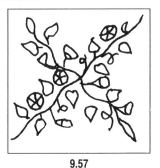

9.57
D Morning Glory—
Nancy Cabot, *Chicago Tribune* 1933

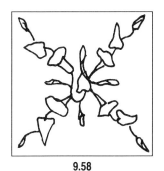

9.58
D Morning Glory—
Ladies Art Company

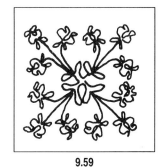

9.59
T Floral—
Spencer Museum of Art

Four Fruits 9.6-9.7

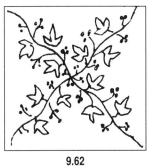

9.62
T Turquoise Berries—
Nancy Cabot, *Chicago Tribune* 1933

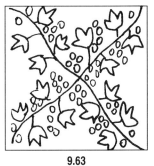

9.63
T Grapevine Block—
Nancy Cabot, *Chicago Tribune* 1937

9.67
T Pomegranate—
from a quilt in Havig/Missouri, pg. 34

9.68
T Cotton Boll—
from a quilt in Texas Heritage
Quilt Soc.

9.72
T Rosebuds—
Nancy Cabot, *Chicago Tribune*

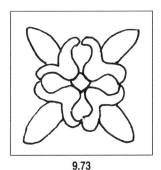

9.73
D Golden Corn—
Hall and Kretsinger, pg. 109

9.74
T Unnamed—
from an album dated 1854

9.75
T Pineapple—
Finley, plate 79

9.76
T Hawaiian Blocks—
Wheeler/Brooks #7053

9.77
T Hospitality—
Sienkeiwicz

9.78
T Unnamed—
from an album dated 1853

9.79
T Unnamed—
from an album dated 1855

Four Hearts 9.8

9.812
T Mary Moore's Double Irish Chain —
Bureau Farmer 1930
Double Irish Cross—McKim. (both
alternated with a pieced Irish Chain
block; see as a pieced design #1017)

9.813
Unnamed—
Comfort September, 1928

9.821
T Good Luck Block—
Nancy Cabot, *Chicago Tribune* 1933
Luck Quilt—*Oklahoma Farmer
and Stockman* 1935
Four Leaf Clover—*Oklahoma Farmer and
Stockman* 1935 (all alternated with four patch,
see pieced design #1006)

9.822
T Good Luck Clover—
Needlecraft 1933

9.825
T Hearts—
unknown clipping ca. 1890

9.826
T Unnamed—
from an album dated 1857

9.83
T Roses and Hearts—
from a quilt ca. 1963, Marston and
Cunningham

9.842
T Eight of Hearts—
Nancy Cabot, *Chicago Tribune* 1933
Sweethearts—
Nancy Cabot, *Chicago Tribune*

9.843
T Double Heart—
unknown clipping ca. 1890
Friendship Quilt—
Ladies Art Company #180

9.844
T Traditional Geometric Design—
Ickis, pg. 47

9.85
T Hearts All Around—
Hearth and Home

9.874
Friendship Quilt—
Kansas City Star 1938
A Heart for Applique—
Kansas City Star 1951

9.875
Sweetheart Quilt—
Capper's Weekly

9.882
T Unnamed—
from an album dated 1854

9.884
T Unnamed—
from an album dated 1852

9.89
T Unnamed—
from an album dated 1850

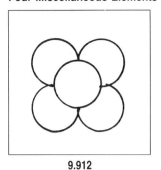

9.912
D Dogwood Applique—
Farmer's Wife 1932
Forget Me Not—
Nancy Cabot, *Chicago Tribune* 1936

9.913
D Friendship Band—
Hearth and Home

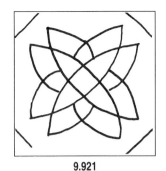

9.921
D Double Poppy—
Nancy Cabot, *Chicago Tribune*

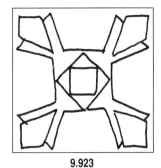

9.923
D Modern Corsage—
Nancy Cabot, *Chicago Tribune* 1936

9.924
D Flemish Tile—
Nancy Cabot, *Chicago Tribune* 1937

9.926
D Weathervane—
Nancy Cabot, *Chicago Tribune*

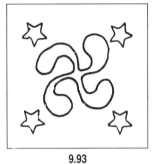

9.93
T Unnamed—
from an album dated 1860

9.941
D Four Chartres Lilies—
Nancy Cabot, *Chicago Tribune* 1936

9.943
D King's Crown—
Nancy Cabot, *Chicago Tribune* 1938

9.945
D Geneva Tassal Flower—
Nancy Cabot, *Chicago Tribune* 1936

9.95
D Rose and Lily Block—
Nancy Cabot, *Chicago Tribune* 1936

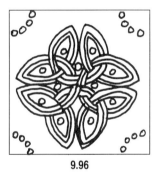

9.96
D Tipperary Tangle—
Nancy Cabot, *Chicago Tribune* 1935

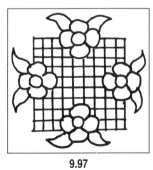

9.97
D Wild Roses and Squares—
Nancy Cabot, *Chicago Tribune* 1934

9.981
D Rock Rose—
Nancy Cabot, *Chicago Tribune* 1937

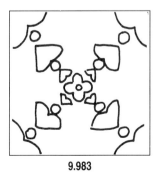

9.983
D Lilac Zinnia—
Nancy Cabot, *Chicago Tribune* 1936

9.99
T Whig Rose Variation—
from a quilt dated 1859 -
Crews/Nebraska

10.12
D Begonia—
Nancy Cabot, *Chicago Tribune* 1934

10.13
T Simple Floral Block—
Nancy Cabot, *Chicago Tribune*
Floral Block—
Nancy Cabot, *Chicago Tribune* 1937

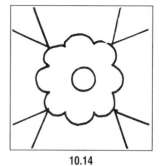

10.14
D Wild Rose Quilt—
Wheeler/Brooks #1974

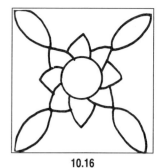

10.16
D California Sunflower—
Ladies Art Company #459

10.22
T Peony and Buds—
Nancy Cabot, *Chicago Tribune* 1938

10.24
T French Rose—
Nancy Cabot, *Chicago Tribune*

10.32
D Star Flowers—
Nancy Cabot, *Chicago Tribune* 1935

10.35
D Daisy Block—
Nancy Cabot, *Chicago Tribune* 1937

10.37
D Rose Point—
Nancy Cabot, *Chicago Tribune* 1933

10.39
D Texas Sunflower—
Nancy Cabot, Grandmother Book
#29

10.42
T Original Rose #3—
Webster, figure 61

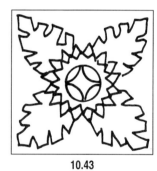

10.43
T Fringed Rose—
Nancy Cabot, *Chicago Tribune* 1935

10.52
T Rose of Sharon—
Herrschner
Wild Rose—
Mrs. Danner

10.53
T Open Dahlia—
name inscribed on a quilt ca. 1870
Shelburne #10.323

10.54
T Rose of Sharon—
McCall's Needlework Winter 1941–2

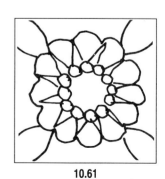

10.61
D Coneflower—
Nancy Cabot, *Chicago Tribune* 1934

10.63
T Unnamed—
from an album dated 1854

10.64
T Bleeding Heart—
Comfort

10.66
T Unnamed—
from an album dated 1853

10.67
T Charter Oak—
Hall and Kretsinger pg. 118

10.68
T Unnamed—
from an album dated 1845

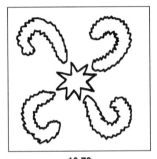

10.72
T Unnamed—
from an album dated 1863

10.74
T Unnamed—
alternates with Feathered Star in
Webster fig. 35

10.76
T Whirling Swastika—
Peto/*American Quilts* pg. 20

10.78
T Prince's Feather—
Mrs. Danner

10.82
D Royal Water Lily—
Nancy Cabot, *Chicago Tribune* 1934

10.83
D African Daisy—
Nancy Cabot, *Chicago Tribune* 1935

10.84
D Honeysuckle—
Nancy Cabot, *Chicago Tribune* 1934

10.85
D Dahlia—
Nancy Cabot, *Chicago Tribune* 1934

10.86
D Paneled Daisy—
Nancy Cabot, *Chicago Tribune* 1937

10.87
D Shasta Daisy—
Hearth and Home

10.89
T Fireworks—
Nancy Cabot, *Chicago Tribune* 1935
Midnight Sky—
Nancy Cabot, *Chicago Tribune* 1938

11.12
T Hearts—
Shelburne Museum

11.15
T Unnamed—
from an album dated 1850

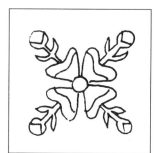

11.21
The Wild Rose—
Capper's Weekly
Conventional Wild Rose—
Hall and Kretsinger, pg. 116

11.22
Topeka Rose—
Hall and Kretsinger, pg. 111

11.23
Hearts and Flowers, Ickis, pg. 128

11.25
Ohio Rose—Carlie Sexton, Mountain
Mist, *Farmer's Wife* October, 1929
Rose of Sharon—*Capper's Weekly*
Yellow Rose of Texas—*Capper's Weekly*
Rose of Sharon—*Farmer's Wife* 1932

11.32
Rose of Sharon Cluster—
Ladies Art Company #6081

11.35
Rose of Sharon—
Hall and Kretsinger pg. 112

11.42
Colonial Rose—
St. Louis Fancy Work

11.45
Bud and Blossom—
The Family 1913

11.52
Prairie Rose—
Nancy Cabot, *Chicago Tribune*

11.55
Colonial Rose—
Sears, Roebuck and Co. 1934

11.62
Louisiana Rose—
Sears, Roebuck and Co. 1934

11.65
Ohio Rose—
Nancy Cabot, *Chicago Tribune* 1933

11.72
Radical Rose—
Hall and Kretsinger pg. 116

11.75
New Rose of Sharon—
Nancy Cabot, *Chicago Tribune* 1936

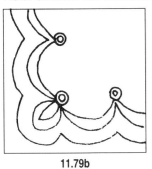

11.79b
The Rose of Sharon—
Mrs. Danner (scalloped edge)

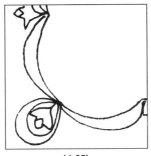

11.25b
Yellow Rose of Texas—
Capper's Weekly

11.42b
Colonial Rose—
Louis Fancy Work

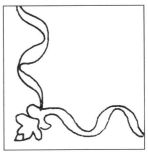

11.32b
Rose of Sharon Cluster—
Ladies Art Company #6081

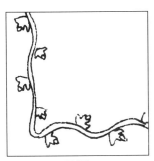

11.25b
Ohio Rose—
Mountain Mist

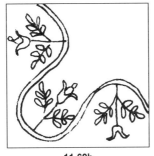

11.62b
Louisiana Rose—
Sears, Roebuck and Co. 1934

11.81
T Unnamed—
from an album dated 1850

11.82
T Unnamed—
from an album dated 1846

11.831
T Combination Rose—Webster
California Rose—Hall and
Kretsinger, pg. 114
Texas Yellow Rose—Hall and
Kretsinger, pg. 114

11.832
T Grandmother's Quilt—
St. Louis Fancywork

11.835
T Pennsylvania Dutch Rose—
Nancy Cabot, *Chicago Tribune* 1933

11.87
T From a quilt ca. 1850 in Safford
& Bishop, pg. 168

11.88
T Irish Rose—
Nancy Cabot, *Chicago Tribune* 1933

11.92
D New Tulip Block—
Nancy Cabot, *Chicago Tribune* 1936

11.95
D Tulips and Buds—
Nancy Cabot, *Chicago Tribune* 1937

11.97
T Unnamed—
from an album dated 1865

12.12
T Rose Cross—
Hall and Kretsinger, pg. 104

12.14
T Rose and Lily—
Nancy Cabot, *Chicago Tribune* 1937
Unnamed—
Modern Priscilla March, 1926

12.18
T Rose Cross—
McKim

12.22
T Pomegranate—
Peto, *American Quilts* pg. 12

12.14
T Jefferson Rose—
from a quilt ca. 1849 in
Ramsey/Tennessee, pg. 7 (Leaves
in corners are alternate blocks)

12.26
T Pomegranate—
Ladies Art Company #6018
Rose and Peony—
Farm and Fireside September, 1929

12.28
T Pomegranate—
Nancy Cabot, *Chicago Tribune* 1937

Four Tulips/Floral Center

12.31
T Ohio Rose—
Hall and Kretsinger

12.33
T Scotch Thistle—
Carlie Sexton

12.35
Geranium Wreath—
Nancy Cabot, *Chicago Tribune* 1937

12.37
T Elderberry Bloom—
Nancy Cabot, *Chicago Tribune* 1938

12.39
T Spiced Pinks—
Nancy Cabot, *Chicago Tribune* 1937

12.41
T Ohio Rose—
Webster
Forget Me Not—
Carlie Sexton

12.42
T Ohio Rose—
Needlecraft Magazine 1926

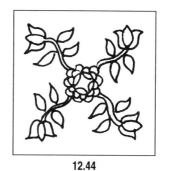

12.44
T Unnamed—
from a quilt in the *Quilt
Engagement Calendar* 1977, plate 2

12.47
D Cyclamen—
Nancy Cabot, *Chicago Tribune* 1935

12.52
T Rose of 1840—
Nancy Cabot, *Chicago Tribune* 1935

12.55
D Oriental Rose—
Nancy Cabot, *Chicago Tribune*

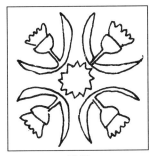

12.57
D Persian Poinsettia—
Nancy Cabot, *Chicago Tribune* 1937

12.59
T Thistle—
Nancy Cabot, *Chicago Tribune* 1937

12.62
T Yellow Indiana Rose—
Nancy Cabot, *Chicago Tribune* 1938

12.63
T Conventional Lily Applique—
Comfort September, 1928

12.65
T Indiana Rose—
Nancy Cabot, *Chicago Tribune* 1933

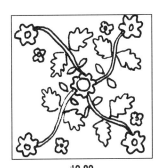

12.68
T Pumpkin—
Ladies Art Company #508

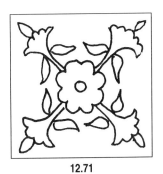

12.71
T New Jersey Rose—
Nancy Cabot, *Chicago Tribune* 1933
Jersey Rose—
Nancy Cabot, *Chicago Tribune* 1937
Jersey Bouquet—
Nancy Cabot, *Chicago Tribune* 1937

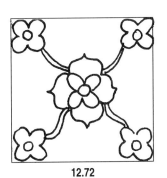

12.72
D Memory Block—
Nancy Cabot, *Chicago Tribune* 1937

12.81
T Unnamed—
from an album dated 1852

12.82
T Unnamed—
from the center of a Cornucopia
from Mrs. Danner (see #38)

12.84
T Democratic Rose—
Carlie Sexton

12.86
T Unnamed—
from a quilt ca. 1840 in Safford and
Bishop, pg. 168

12.87
T California Rose—
Bishop/Knopf, pg. 165

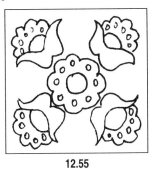

12.88
T English Rose—
Hall and Kretsinger Page 22

Floral Centers/Four Elements 10-13

12.91
T Sunburst and Rose of Sharon—
from a quilt in Safford and Bishop,
pg. 193

12.93
T Double Tulip—
Webster, plate 30
Double Peony and Wild Rose—
Hall and Kretsinger, pg. 109

12.95
T Irish Beauty—
Mrs. Danner

12.97
T Oriental Poppy—
Kretsinger in Hall and Kretsinger

Four Fruits (& Miscellaneous)/Floral Center 13

13.12
T Unnamed—
in *Modern Priscilla* 1925

13.13
T Foundation Rose and Pine
Tree—
Shelburne Museum

13.14
T Cherry—
Kimball

13.2
T Unnamed—
quilt in MacDowell/Michigan

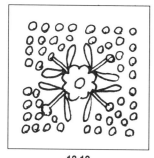

13.31
T Watermelon—
Horton/*Social Fabric*, pg. 24

13.32
T Melon Patch—
Ickis, pg. 127

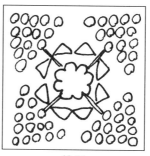

13.41
T Mrs. Harris's Colonial Rose—
Hall and Kretsinger, pg. 111

13.43
T Edith Hall's Rose—
Ramsey/Tennessee

13.52
T Unnamed—
from an album dated 1863

13.54
T Planet Jupiter—
Nancy Cabot, *Chicago Tribune* 1936

13.6
T Unnamed—
from an album dated 1853

13.7
T Unnamed—
from an album dated 1847

14.11
T Unnamed

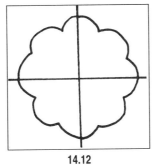

14.12
Autograph—
from a quilt ca. 1935 in Arkansas
book

14.13
Unnamed—
Needlecraft 1940

14.14
T Unnamed—
from a quilt ca. 1850 in
Havig/Missouri

14.16
T Friendship—
Safford and Bishop, pg. 193

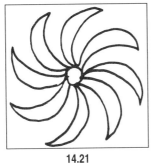

14.21
D Windblown Daisy—
Nancy Cabot, *Chicago Tribune* 1933

14.22
T Unnamed—
from an album dated 1850

14.23
T Zinnia—
Nancy Cabot, *Chicago Tribune* 1934

14.24
D Yellow Hemstitch—
Nancy Cabot, *Chicago Tribune*

14.25
D Blue Meadow Flower—
Nancy Cabot, *Chicago Tribune* 1937

14.26
D Double Dahlia Block—
Nancy Cabot, *Chicago Tribune* 1937

14.3
T Star Flower—
Nancy Cabot, *Chicago Tribune* 1933

14.41
T Snowflake—
Nancy Cabot, *Chicago Tribune* 1934

14.42
T Bouquet Quilt Block—
Comfort

14.52
D Tulip Wreath—
Nancy Cabot, *Chicago Tribune* 1933

14.54
D Windblown Tulip—
Webster

14.57
T Unnamed—
from an album dated 1847

14.59
T Unnamed—
from an album dated 1863

14.61
T The Rose Bud—
Mrs. Danner, Books 1 & 2
Whig Rose—
Mrs. Danner, Books 1 & 2

14.62
T Whig Rose—
Aunt Martha, *Prize-Winning Quilts*

14.63
T Whig Rose—
Ramsey/Tennessee

14.64
T Whig Rose—
The Household ca. 1912
Rose Bud Wreath—
Ladies Art Company #498

14.65
T Mrs. Kretsinger's Rose—
Hall and Kretsinger, pg. 116

14.66
T Yellow Rose—
Nancy Cabot, *Chicago Tribune* 1933

14.67
T Whig Rose—
Peto, *American Quilts*

14.71
D Mimosa Wreath—
Nancy Cabot, *Chicago Tribune* 1936

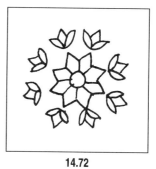

14.72
Ipswich Bouquet—
Nancy Cabot, *Chicago Tribune* 1938

14.73
T The Tulip Pattern—
Ladies Home Journal 1908

14.74
T Conventional Rose—
Hall and Kretsinger, pg. 109

14.75
T Rose of Tennessee—
Nancy Cabot, *Chicago Tribune* 1933

14.76
T Roses and Tulips—
Nancy Cabot, *Chicago Tribune* 1933

14.77
T Unnamed—
from an album dated 1846

14.78
T Unnamed—
from a quilt ca. 1850 in Spencer
Museum of Art

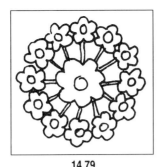

14.79
D Lavender Lace Flower—
Nancy Cabot, *Chicago Tribune* 1934

14.81
T Rose of Sharon—
Hall and Kretsinger, pg. 112

14.82
T Unnamed—
found in several mid-nineteenth
century quilts primarily from Garrard
County, Kentucky

14.83
T Eight Pointed Star with
Sprigs of Berries—
Sienkeiwicz

14.841
T Rose of Sharon—
from a quilt ca. 1850 in Kimball, pg.
146

14.843
T The Ladies' Dream—
Mrs. Danner

14.844
T Pumpkin Blossom—
Nancy Cabot, *Chicago Tribune*

14.847
T Unnamed—
from a quilt in Ramsey/Tennessee

14.848
T Pomegranate—
from a quilt ca. 1890 in
Uncoverings 1984

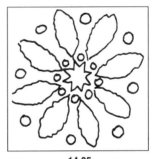

14.85
T Oak Leaf and Cherries—
from a quilt Texas Heritage Quilt
Society

14.87
T Unnamed—
from an album dated 1846

14.91
T Unnamed—
Farm and Fireside

14.93
T Unnamed—
from a quilt ca. 1850 in Safford and
Bishop, pg. 104

14.95
T Double Hearts—
from a quilt dated 1853 in Safford
and Bishop, pg. 193

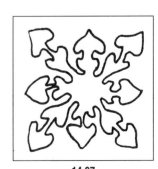

14.97
T The United Hearts—
Capper's Weekly

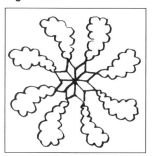

15.12

T Princess Feather—
Ladies Art Company #325
Star and Plumes—
Hall and Kretsinger

15.14

T Washington Feather—
Nancy Cabot, *Chicago Tribune* 1938

15.16

T Princess Feathers—
Safford and Bishop

15.18

T Princess Feather—
Finley

15.22

T Feather Rose—
Hall and Kretsinger

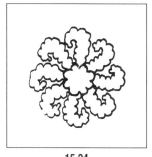

15.24

T Princess Feather—
Nancy Cabot, *Chicago Tribune* 1933

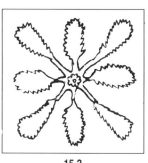

15.3

T Princess Feathers—
Webster

15.4

T Ben Hur's Chariot Wheel—
Hall and Kretsinger
Princess Feather—
Hall and Kretsinger

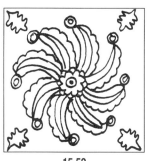

15.52

T Princess Feather with
Oak Leaves—
Holstein/Kentucky

15.54

T Princess Feather—
from a quilt dated 1873 in Spencer
Museum of Art

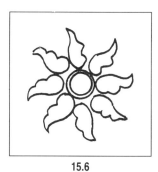

15.6

T Unnamed—
from an album dated 1846

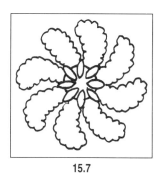

15.7

T Cucumber—
Roberson/North Carolina

15.8

T Unnamed—
The Farmer's Wife October, 1929

15.91

T Snowflake—
from a quilt ca. 1860

15.93

T Unnamed—
from a quilt dated 1872 in
Roberson/North Carolina, pg. 90
Carolina Medallion—
Uncoverings 1987

15.98

T Unnamed—
from an album dated 1854

16.1
Hawthorne Berries—
Nancy Cabot, *Chicago Tribune* 1935

16.2
D Tangerine—
Nancy Cabot, *Chicago Tribune* 1936

16.3
T Grape and Morning Glory—
Carlie Sexton

16.4
D Honeysuckle—
Nancy Cabot, *Chicago Tribune* 1935

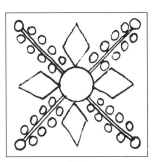

16.5
T Tree of Life—
People's Popular Monthly 1915

16.55
T Martha's Vineyard—
Mountain Mist #28

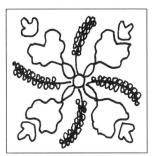

16.61
T Currants and Cockscombs—
Webster

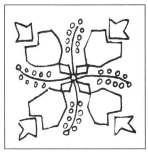

16.62
T Coxcombs and Currants—
Nancy Cabot, *Chicago Tribune* 1935
Spray and Buds—
Nancy Cabot, *Chicago Tribune* 1935

16.63
T Cockscomb and Currants—
from a quilt ca. 1890 in
Ramsey/Tennessee

16.64
T Oak Leaf Variant—
from a quilt ca. 1860 in
Holstein/Kentucky, pg. 39

16.65
T Flowering Almond—
Comfort
Chestnut Berry—
Comfort February, 1926

16.66
T Poinsettia—
Finley, plate 73

16.67
T Grapes and Oak Leaf—
Roan/Goschenhoppen

16.68
T Cockscombs and Currants—
from a quilt ca 1870
Ramsey/Tennessee

16.69
T Unnamed—
Lasansky, *In The Heart of
Pennsylvania* pg. 35

16.7
Tomato Flower—
Denver Art Museum

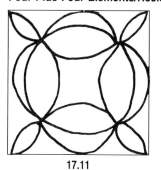

17.11

T Hickory Leaf—Ladies Art Company #70; Job's Patience—*Country Life* February, 19; Orange Peel—Carlie Sexton in *Country Gentleman* July, 1926; The Reel—Finley; Compass—Carlie Sexton; Order #11—McKim; Orange Slices—Shelburne Museum; Oak Leaf—Beth Gutcheon. (See as a pieced design #3110.)

17.12

T Irish Chain—
Hearth and Home

17.13

T Hickory Leaf—
Hearth and Home

17.14

T Unnamed—
from an album dated 1847

17.15

T Soul Knot—
Hearth and Home

17.16

T California Oak Leaf—
Ladies Art Company #497

17.17

T Bear Paw—
Mrs. Danner, ca. 1930
Oak Leaf and Reel—
Mrs. Danner, ca. 1970

17.18

T True Lover's Knot—
Carlie Sexton

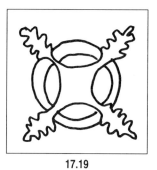

17.19

T California Oak Leaf—
Needlecraft 1929

17.20

T Oak Leaf—
Ickis

17.21

T Hero's Crown—
Finley, pg. 124

17.22

T Fredonia Oak Leaf—
Mrs. Danner

17.23

T Crown of Oaks—
Nancy Cabot, *Chicago Tribune* 1937

17.24

T Oak Leaf—
possibly *Household Magazine*,
ca. 1920

17.25

T Oak Leaf and Acorn—
Hall and Kretsinger pg. 118

17.26

T Unnamed—
from a quilt ca. 1835 in the
Shelburne Museum

17.27
T Oak Leaf Pattern—
Country Life February, 1923

17.32
T Harrison Rose—
Ladies Art Company #187

17.33
T Nebraska Oak Leaf—
Wheeler/Brooks #5830

17.34
T Rose of Sharon—
Carlie Sexton

17.35
T Marigold—
Nancy Cabot, *Chicago Tribune* 1937
Rose in a Ring—
Aunt Martha, *Prize-Winning Quilts*
Ragged Robin—
Mrs. Danner

17.36
T Poppy—
Rural New Yorker

17.4
T Unnamed—
from a quilt ca. 1840

17.51
T Pineapple—
Horton/*Social Fabric*, pg. 38

17.52
T Prickly Pear—
Texas Heritage Quilt Society

17.53
T Unnamed—
Texas Heritage Quilt Society

17.6
T Sunburst—
from a quilt ca. 1892 in Davis

17.72
T Unnamed—
from an album dated 1845

17.73
T Oak Leaf Variation—
Safford and Bishop, pg. 162

17.81
Rose Point—
Nancy Cabot, *Chicago Tribune*

17.82
Aunt Flora's Bouquet—
Nancy Cabot, *Chicago Tribune* 1936

17.83
D Scotch Thistle—
Nancy Cabot, *Chicago Tribune* 1935

18.11
Cock's Comb—
Ickis pg. 72

18.13
Rose of the Wilderness—
Comfort

18.14
T Spiced Pinks—
Nancy Cabot, *Chicago Tribune* 1933
Pinks—
Nancy Cabot, *Chicago Tribune* 1938

18.22
T Combination Rose—
Carlie Sexton

18.24
T Democrat Rose—
The Household ca. 1912

18.32
T Unnamed—
Comfort February, 1926

18.33
T Spice Pink—
Finley, plate 64
Tea Rose—
Carlie Sexton

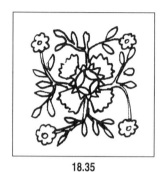

18.35
T The Whig Rose—Finley, plate 19
Democrat Rose—Hall and Kretsinger 114
Antique Rose—Mrs. Danner

18.37
T Tea Rose—
Nancy Cabot, *Chicago Tribune* 1935

18.4
T Rose Tree Block—
Carlie Sexton, *Old Fashioned
Quilts*, pg. 21

18.5
T Democratic Rose—
Nancy Cabot, *Chicago Tribune* 1936

18.6
T Tea Rose—
Nancy Cabot, *Chicago Tribune* 1933

18.72
T Running Rose—
Farm and Fireside September, 1929

18.74
T Antique Rose—Hall and Kretsinger
T Old Spice Pink—*Farm Journal* 1949
Similar block called Harvest
Rose—*Comfort*

18.76
T Rose of Sharon—
Hall and Kretsinger, pg. 113

18.78
T Unnamed—
from a quilt in the *Quilt
Engagement Calendar*

78

Four Plus Four Elements/Combs 18

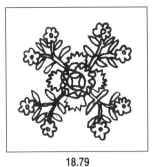

18.79
T Whig Rose—
Bishop/Knopf, pg. 162

18.81
T California Rose—
Bishop/Knopf, pg. 164

18.83
T Rose of Sharon—
Holstein/Kentucky, pg. 70

18.85
T Unnamed—
Fox, *Small Endearments*, pg. 33

18.88
T Rose of Sharon Variation—
Horton, *Social Fabric*, pg. 22

18.92
T Whig Rose—
Ickis, pg. 134

18.94
T Unnamed—
Kansas Quilt Project #Ha140

18.96
T Unnamed—
Fox/Utah pg.24

Four Plus Four Elements 16-25

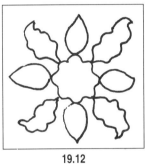

19.12
T Rose and Oak Leaf—
Ickis, pg. 5

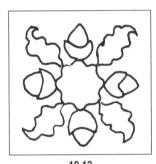

19.13
T Acorn and Oak Leaf—
Mountain Mist Oak
Leaves and Acorns—
Nancy Cabot, *Chicago Tribune* 1933

19.15
T Mahoning Rose—
Nancy Cabot, *Chicago Tribune* 1936

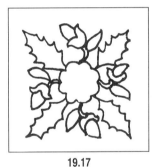

19.17
T Kentucky Rose—
Nancy Cabot, *Chicago Tribune* 1934

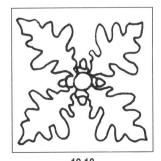

19.18
T The Oak Leaf—
Nancy Page (from the Leaf
series quilt)

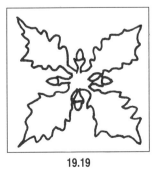

19.19
T Oak Leaf and Acorn—
unknown clipping ca. 1890

19.22
T Oak Leaf—
from a quilt ca. 1860

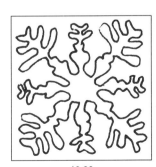

19.23
T Red Oak Block—
Nancy Cabot, *Chicago Tribune* 1937

19.24
T Forest—
from a quilt dated 1861 in the Art
Institute of Chicago

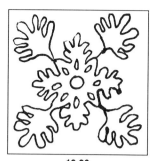

19.26
T Unnamed—
from an album dated 1844

19.31
T Unnamed—
from a quilt ca. 1850
Cochise County—
Ladies Circle Patchwork Quilts
(similar)

19.33
T Unnamed—
from a quilt in the *Quilt
Engagement Calendar* 1984,
plate 46

19.35
T Tulip Cross—
Woodard & Greenstein, plate 81
Princess Feather and Tulip—
Safford and Bishop pg. 193

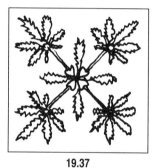

19.37
T Mountain Laurel—
Hall and Kretsinger, pg. 109

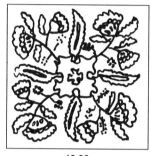

19.38
T Cockscomb—
Kimball

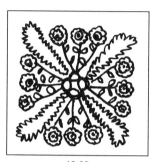

19.39
T Unnamed—
Lasansky, *Pieced by Mother*

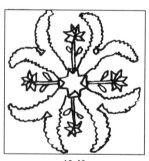

19.42
T Cactus—
Roan/Goschenhoppen

19.43
T Flowering Fan—
Quilt Engagement Calendar 1977,
plate 35

19.44
T Jester's Plume—
Quilter's Newsletter Magazine #177

19.46
T Star and Plume—
Finley, pg. 63

19.52
T Tulip Design—
Ickis, pg. 109

19.54
T The Rose and Thorn—
Quilter's Newsletter Magazine #191,
pg. 53

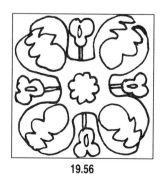

19.56
T Persian Block—
Nancy Cabot, *Chicago Tribune* 1937

19.58
T Conventional Applique—
Webster

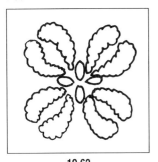

19.62
T   The Feather—
from a quilt ca. 1890 in
Uncoverings 1984

19.64
T   Unnamed—
Safford and Bishop, pg. 194

19.72
T   Unnamed—
Lasansky, *Pieced by Mother*, pg. 51
Poppy Applique—
Woodard and Greenstein, Crib
Quilts, pg. 54

19.74
T   Unnamed—
Woodard and Greenstein, pg. 51

19.75
T   Coxcomb—
Quilter's Newsletter Magazine #165,
pg. 24

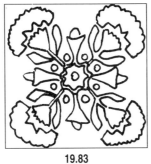

19.83
T   Cock's Comb—
Woodard and Greenstein, *Crib
Quilts*, plate 85

19.85
T   Unnamed

19.9
T   Oriental Poppy—
Hall and Kretsinger
Similar pattern named Pink Rose—
Comfort

20.12
T   Rose of Sharon—
Nancy Cabot, *Chicago Tribune*

20.14
Mountain Laurel—
Nancy Cabot, *Chicago Tribune* 1935

20.18
D   Oregon Daisy—
Nancy Cabot, *Chicago Tribune*

20.22
D   Double Dahlia—
Nancy Cabot, *Chicago Tribune* 1938

20.24
D   Full Blown Rose—
Nancy Cabot, *Chicago Tribune* 1937

20.26
T   Clover Block—
Ladies Art Company #499

20.31
D   California Poppy—
Nancy Cabot, *Chicago Tribune* 1934

20.32
D   Cosmos—
Nancy Cabot, *Chicago Tribune* 1934

20.33
T Rose of Sharon—
Ickis, pg. 121

20.35
T Forest Bouquet—
Nancy Cabot, *Chicago Tribune* 1938

20.36
T Sadie's Choice—
Nancy Cabot, *Chicago Tribune* 1937

20.37
T Sadie's Choice—Carlie Sexton
Mexican Tea Rose—Nancy Cabot,
Chicago Tribune 1935
Balm of Gilead—Nancy Cabot,
Chicago Tribune
Peony—Hall and Kretsinger, pg. 111

20.38
T Full Blown Rose—
Nancy Cabot, *Chicago Tribune* 1933
June Rose—
Nancy Cabot, *Chicago Tribune* 1937

20.42
T Portulaca—
Nancy Cabot, *Chicago Tribune*

20.44
T Tulip—
from a quilt dated 1888,
Roberson/North Carolina, pg. 174

20.52
T Unnamed—
unknown clipping 1916

20.54
T Rose of Sharon—
Finley

20.62
Bachelor's Buttons—
Nancy Cabot, *Chicago Tribune* 1935

20.64
D Appliqued Lotus—
Nancy Cabot, *Chicago Tribune* 1936

20.66
T The Tulip—
Country Life February, 1923

20.68
T Rose of Sharon—
Source not found

20.69
T Unnamed

20.72
T Sharon Rose—
Rural New Yorker

20.8
D Flowered Cross—
Nancy Cabot, *Chicago Tribune* 1934
Five Roses—
Nancy Cabot, *Chicago Tribune* 1938

20.92
T Democrat Rose—
Source not found

20.94
T Rose of Sharon—
from a quilt ca. 1860, in *Kentucky
Quilts*, pg. 37

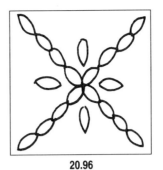

20.96
D String of Beads—Aunt Martha
Studios Beads—Nancy Cabot,
Chicago Tribune 1933
Poinsettia—Aunt Martha

20.97
T Diamond Vine—
Nancy Cabot, *Chicago Tribune* 1936

20.98
D Lavender Puzzle—
Nancy Cabot, *Chicago Tribune* 1933

21.12
T Unnamed—
from an album dated 1852

21.13
T Poinsettia—
Webster (alternated with #33.13)

21.14
T Dogwood—
Rural New Yorker

21.22
T Laurel Leaves—
Safford and Bishop, pg. 158

21.24
T Pine Tree—
Needlecraft Magazine 1933

21.26
T Goldenrod—
Nancy Cabot, *Chicago Tribune* 1935

21.28
T Crossed Laurel Spray—
Sienkeiwicz

21.32
T Delphinium—
Nancy Cabot, *Chicago Tribune*

21.34
D Fuschia—
Nancy Cabot, *Chicago Tribune* 1937

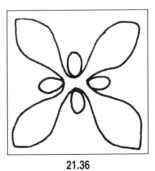

21.36
T Horse Chestnut—
Nancy Cabot, *Chicago Tribune* 1935

21.38
D Appliqued Rose Petal—
Ickis, pg. 7

21.42
D Virginia Stock—
Nancy Cabot, *Chicago Tribune* 1934

21.44
D Clematis—
Nancy Cabot, *Chicago Tribune* 1934

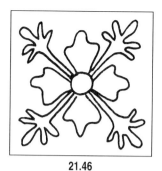

21.46
T Mexican Rose—
Hall and Kretsinger, pg. 109

21.52
T Unnamed—
from an album dated 1859

21.54
T Tulip Quilt—
Modern Priscilla 1925
Tulip Cross—
Ladies Art Company #A261

21.56
T Holland Tulip—
Nancy Cabot, *Chicago Tribune* 1937

21.58
T Pennsylvania Tulip—
Country Home ca. 1935

21.62
D Peony—
Nancy Cabot, *Chicago Tribune* 1934

21.64
T Unnamed—
from an album dated 1855

21.66
D Swordbush—
Nancy Cabot, *Chicago Tribune* 1936

21.68
D Passion Flower—
Nancy Cabot, *Chicago Tribune*

21.72
Unnamed—
Modern Priscilla March, 1926
Hearts and Flowers—
Nancy Cabot, *Chicago Tribune* 1935

21.74
D Tulip Applique—
Wheeler/Brooks

21.82
Tulip Wreath—
Nancy Cabot, *Chicago Tribune* 1934
Tulip Circle—
Nancy Cabot, *Chicago Tribune*

21.84
Yellow Lily Block—
Nancy Cabot, *Chicago Tribune* 1936

21.86
Lilies of France—
Nancy Cabot, *Chicago Tribune* 1936

21.88
D Roses in the Snow—
Country Home ca. 1935

21.92
D March Tulip—
Sophie LaCroix

21.94
D Floral Wreath—
Grandma Dexter
Rio Wreath—
Nancy Cabot, *Chicago Tribune*

21.96
D Oriental Magnolias—
Nancy Cabot, *Chicago Tribune*

22.12
T Mexican Rose—
Nancy Cabot, *Chicago Tribune* 1933

22.13
T Mexican Rose—
McKim

22.15
T Mexican Rose—
Hall and Kretsinger, pg. 116

22.2
T Mrs. Brown's Peony—
Mrs. Danner

22.32
T Meadow Daisy—
Nancy Cabot, *Chicago Tribune* 1933

22.34
D Dogwood Block—
Nancy Cabot, *Chicago Tribune* 1935

22.41
T Mexican Rose—
Ladies Art Company #186
Aztec Rose—
Nancy Cabot, *Chicago Tribune* 1937

22.42
T Mexican Rose—
Webster, fig. 37

22.43
T Unnamed—
from an album dated 1855

22.44
T Meadow Daisy—
Finley, pg. 125
Black-Eyed Susan—
Hall and Kretsinger

22.45
T Forget Me Not—
Modern Priscilla, 917

22.47
T Unnamed—
from an album dated 1847

22.51
Tulip—
Comfort

22.52
D Sweet Peas—
Nancy Cabot, *Chicago Tribune* 1935

22.54
D Iris—
Capper's Weekly
Similar pattern called Bearded Iris—
Hinson/Quilting Manual

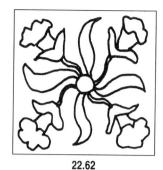

22.62
D Jonquils—
Nancy Cabot, *Chicago Tribune* 1934

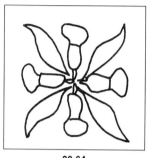

22.64
D Tassel Flower—
Nancy Cabot, *Chicago Tribune* 1934

22.66
D Mexican Rosebud—
Nancy Cabot, *Chicago Tribune* 1934

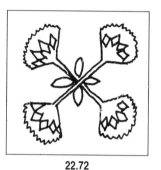

22.72
T Coxcomb—
Shelburne Museum

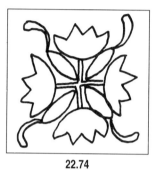

22.74
D Cleome—
Nancy Cabot, *Chicago Tribune* 1934

22.83
D Four Lotus Blossoms—
Nancy Cabot, *Chicago Tribune* 1938

22.85
Easter Lilies—
Hall and Kretsinger, pg. 111

23.12
T Oak Leaf—
Finley, plate 20

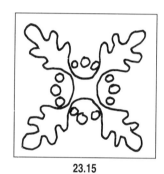

23.15
T Oak Leaf and Cherries—
Hall and Kretsinger, pg. 119

23.17
T Oak Leaf—
Needlecraft Magazine 1930

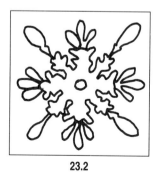

23.2
T Single Carnation—
Comfort

23.3
T Cockscomb—
Comfort
Lemon Lily—
Comfort

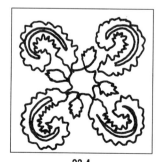

23.4
T Prince's Feather—
Comfort

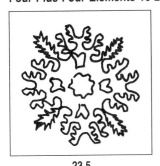

23.5
T Unnamed—
from an album dated 1848

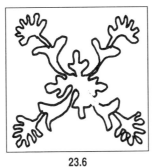

23.6
T Unnamed—
from a quilt in the *Quilt
Engagement Calendar* 1975,
plate 26

23.7
T Unnamed—
from an album dated 1846

24.1
D Valentine—
Needlecraft Magazine 1933

24.2
T Unnamed—
from an album

24.3
D Virginia Stock—
Nancy Cabot, *Chicago Tribune* 1934

24.4
T Double Hearts—
Sienkeiwicz

24.5
T Hearts—
Art Insitute of Chicago

24.6
T Cactus Design—
St. Louis Fancy Work #1214

24.7
T Unnamed—
from a quilt in the *Quilt
Engagement Calendar* 1991,
plate 19

24.82
T Hearts and Diamonds—
Nancy Cabot, *Chicago Tribune* 1936

24.84
T Unnamed—
from an album dated 1865

24.86
T Hearts and Diamonds in
Applique —
Kansas City Star 1944

25.12
T Trumpet Vine—
Sienkeiwicz, *Spoken Without a Word*

25.14
T Unnamed—
from an album dated 1850

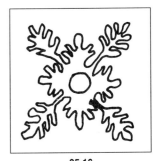

25.16
T Unnamed—
from an album dated 1852

25.18
T Unnamed—
from an album dated 1847

25.21
D Tulip Swirl—
Boag kit

25.22
North Carolina Rose—
Ickis, pg. 96

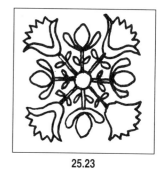

25.23
T The Lotus Flower—
Nancy Cabot, *Chicago Tribune*

25.24
D Four Tulips—
Nancy Cabot, *Chicago Tribune* 1935

25.26
T Conventional Tulips—
Webster

25.27
Garden of Light—
Nancy Cabot, *Chicago Tribune* 1938

25.3
D Farmer's Barometer—
Nancy Cabot, *Chicago Tribune* 1936

25.4
D Verbena—
Nancy Cabot, *Chicago Tribune* 1934

25.5
D Fringed Tulips—
Nancy Cabot, *Chicago Tribune* 1935

25.6
D Lilacs—
Nancy Cabot, *Chicago Tribune* 1935

25.7
D Leaves in the Wind—
Nancy Cabot, *Chicago Tribune* 1935

25.82
Spice Pinks—
Mrs. Danner 1934. See as a pieced
block #2527

25.84
Sweetheart Garden—
Nancy Cabot, *Chicago Tribune* 1933
See variations of this structure
classified as pieced designs
#2525—2528

25.86
Posies Around the Square—
Needlecraft Magazine 7/1934

25.9
T Grandmother's
Engagement Ring—
Mountain Mist. See #91 and as a
pieced pattern #2529

26.12
D Shamrock—
Kansas City Star 1932

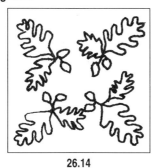

26.14
T Oak Leaf Wreath—
Ickis, pg. 54

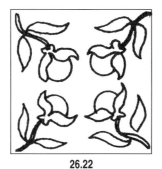

26.22
Rose of Lemoine—
Nancy Cabot, *Chicago Tribune*

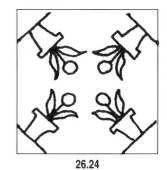

26.24
D Winter Garden—
Nancy Cabot, *Chicago Tribune* 1937

26.32
D Tulip Square—
Wilkinson

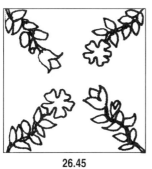

26.34
D Tulip—
Aunt Martha

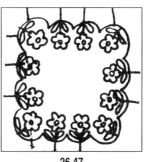

26.36
D Tulip—
Webster design in *Ladies Home Journal* August, 1911

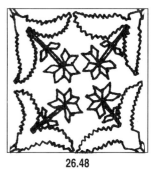

26.42
Rose Spray Square—
Wilkinson

26.44
T Wild Rose Design—
Wilkinson

26.45
D Wild Rose Design—
Modern Priscilla 1925

26.47
D Garden Paths—
Nancy Cabot, *Chicago Tribune* 1937

26.48
T Unnamed—
Lazansky, *Pieced by Mother*, plate 50

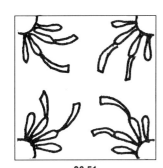

26.51
D Daisy Applique—
Hall and Kretsinger, pg. 104

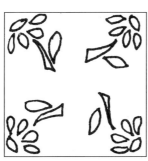

26.52
D Daisy—
Carlie Sexton

26.53
D The Field Daisy—
Webster design in *Ladies Home Journal* August, 1911

26.62
D Pansies—
Nancy Cabot, *Chicago Tribune* 1938

26.63
D Poinsettia—
Grandmother Clark

26.64
D Dancing Daffodil—
Mountain Mist

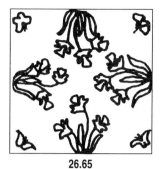

26.65
D Daffodils and Butterflies—
Webster design, *Ladies Home Journal* August, 1911

26.66
D Water Lilies—
Rainbow stamped block #465B

26.67
D Iris—
Webster design, *Ladies Home Journal* August, 1911

26.68
D Iris—
Nancy Cabot, *Chicago Tribune* 1935

26.69
D Iris—
Webster design, *Ladies Home Journal* August, 1911

26.72
D Unnamed—
Nancy Cabot, *Chicago Tribune*

26.73
D Sunshine—
Webster design, *Ladies Home Journal* August, 1911

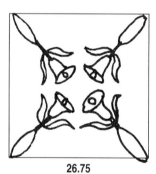

26.75
D Morning Glory Net—
Nancy Cabot, *Chicago Tribune* 1937

26.82
T Watermelon—
Horton/*Social Fabric*, pg. 24

26.84
Autograph Quilt—
from a quilt ca. 1925 in Arkansas
Quilters Guild

26.86
D Hearts and Flowers—
From a quilt dated 1937 in *North Carolina Quilts*, pg. 77

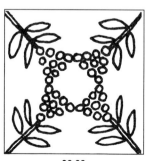

26.92
T Cherry—
Carlie Sexton

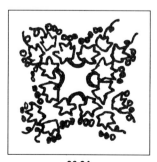

26.94
T Grapes and Vines—
Webster, fig. 66

26.96
T Unnamed—
from an album dated 1848

27.12

T Chrysthanthemum—Ladies Art Company #408; Friendship Ring—McKim; Aster—McKim; Grandmother's Sunbonnet—*Prairie Farmer*; Grandmother's Sunburst—*Wallace's Farmer* 10/12/1928 See as a pieced pattern #3488

27.13

T Aster—
Meeker See as a pieced pattern #3472

27.14

T Sunflower—
Home Art
Landon Sunflower—
Kansas City Star 9/12/1936 See as a pieced pattern #3473

27.15

T China Aster—*Rural New Yorker* 1930
Aster—
Nancy Cabot, *Chicago Tribune* 1933
See as a pieced pattern #3474 and #3485

27.22

T Unnamed—
from an album dated 1847

27.24

D Sunflower—
Nancy Cabot, *Chicago Tribune* 1933
Kansas Sunflower—
Nancy Cabot, *Chicago Tribune* 1938 See as a pieced pattern #3459

27.3

D Dresden Plate—
Mountain Mist See as a pieced pattern #3489.5

27.4

D Sunflower—
Needlecraft Magazine 1931 See as a pieced pattern #3492

27.5

D Love in the Mist—
Nancy Cabot, *Chicago Tribune* 1934

27.62

D Mountain Star—
Mountain Mist

27.64

D Sparkling Star—
Rainbow

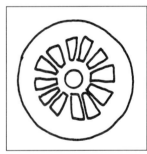

27.7

T Fortune's Wheel—
Hearth and Home

27.81

D Double Poppy—
Nancy Cabot, *Chicago Tribune*
See as a pieced pattern #3460

27.83

T Unnamed—
from an album dated 1855

27.85

D Kansas Sunflower—
Nancy Cabot, *Chicago Tribune* 1936

27.87

D Pinwheel Bouquet—
Nancy Cabot, *Chicago Tribune* 1935

28.12
T Tulip Block—
Ladies Art Company #65
Tulip—
Hearth and Home

28.13
T Dutch Tulip—
Nancy Cabot, *Chicago Tribune* 1935

28.15
T Single Tulip—
Hearth and Home

28.16
Tulip—
from a quilt dated 1932
in *North Carolina Quilts*

28.17
T Anna's Irish Tulip—
Hall and Kretsinger, pg. 122

28.18
T Colonial Tulip—
Hall and Kretsinger, pg. 122

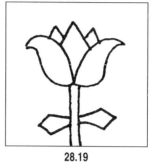

28.19
T Tulip Applique—
McKim in *Kansas City Star* 1929

28.2
D Pride of the Garden—
Wheeler/Brooks

28.32
T Anna Bauersfeld's Tulip—
Hall and Kretsinger, pg. 122

28.33
T Tulip—
from a quilt ca. 1875
in *North Carolina Quilts*, pg. 68

28.34
T Tulip and Sun—
from a quilt ca. 1890
in *North Carolina Quilts*, pg 69

28.36
T Unnamed—
Aunt Martha, *Prize-Winning Quilts*

28.37
T Appliqued Tulip—
Wheeler/Brooks

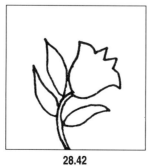

28.42
T Tulip—
Nancy Cabot, *Chicago Tribune*

28.44
T Unnamed—
from an album dated 1860

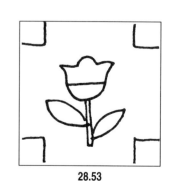

28.53
Tiger Lily—
Farmer's Wife 1932 (alternated with
Irish Chain block)

28.54
D Tulip—
Sophie LaCroix

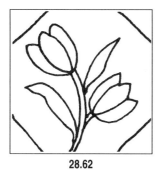

28.62
D Tulips—
Nancy Cabot, *Chicago Tribune* 1935

28.66
D Tulip Garden—
Farmer's Wife 1937

28.67
D Unnamed—
Needlecraft Magazine 1940

28.68
T Unnamed—
from an album dated 1865

28.7
D Bell Flower—
Nancy Cabot, *Chicago Tribune* 1937

29.12
T Tulip—
from a quilt 1875–1900 in
North Carolina Quilts, pg. 66

29.14
T Tulip—
Nancy Cabot, *Chicago Tribune*

29.16
D Unnamed—
Aunt Martha

29.18
T Tulips—
source?

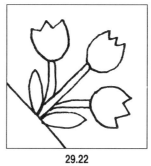

29.22
T Tulips—
Nancy Cabot, *Chicago Tribune*

29.24
T Tiger Lily—
Hall and Kretsinger, pg. 118

29.25
T Mountain Lily—
Elizabeth Daingerfield,
"Patch Quilts and Philosophy"

29.26
Grandmother's Flower Quilt—
Nancy Cabot 1943

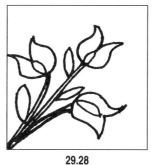

29.28
T Unnamed—
from an album dated 1852

29.33
T Single Tulip—
Webster, plate 35

29.35
T The Tulip Pattern—
Household Magazine

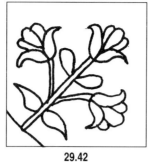

29.42
T Conventional Tulip—
Webster

29.43
T Regal Lily—
Ladies Art Company

29.44
T Rare Old Tulip—
Nancy Cabot, *Chicago Tribune* 1933

29.45
T June Lily—
Rural New Yorker

29.46
T Tiger Lily—
Finley, plate 37

29.47
T Original Tiger Lily—
Nancy Cabot, *Chicago Tribune* 1933

29.48
T Conventional Tulip—
Mountain Mist

29.49
T Rare Old Tulip—
Grandmother Clark Book 20, 1931

29.52
T Dutch Tulips—
from a quilt ca. 1890
in *Quilts of Tennessee*, pg. 1

29.53
T Tulip—
Aunt Martha

29.55
T Rare Old Tulip—
Comfort

29.62
T Tulip—
Wilkinson
Triple Tulip—
Hinson

29.66
T Unnamed—
Aunt Martha, *Prize-Winning Quilts*

29.7
T Cotton Boll—
Art Institute of Chicago catalog

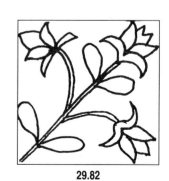

29.82
T Antique Tiger Lily—
Nancy Cabot, *Chicago Tribune* 1933

94

29.83
T Lily of the Valley—
Ladies Art Company #54

29.84
T Lily Quilt—
Nancy Cabot, *Chicago Tribune* 1938

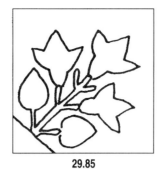

29.85
T White Day Lily—
Nancy Cabot *Chicago Tribune* 1935

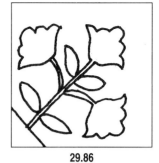

29.86
T Potted Rose Bush—
Nancy Cabot, *Chicago Tribune* 1938

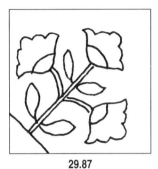

29.87
T Tiger Lily—
Nancy Cabot, *Chicago Tribune* 1933

29.89
T Conventional Tulip—
Country Home ca. 1935

29.91
T Tulip Plant—
Boag kit

29.92
T Tulip Design—
Farmer's Wife 10/1929

29.93
T Tulips—
Kansas City Star 1942
(rectangular block)

29.94
T Three Tulips—
Farm and Fireside September, 1929

29.95
D Tulip—
Carlie Sexton

29.962
T Tulips in Applique—
Comfort

29.964
T Early Tulips—
Nancy Cabot, *Chicago Tribune* 1937

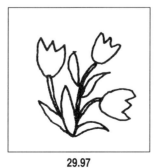

29.97
D Tulip Pillow—
Wheeler/Brooks #7242

29.98
D Tulips in Applique—
Comfort

29.99
D Early Tulips—
Nancy Cabot, *Chicago Tribune* 1937

Bouquets 28-35/Tulips 28-30

30.12
T Unnamed—
from a repeat block quilt,
19th century

30.13
T Stylized Tulip—
Kimball, pg. 131

30.15
T Unnamed—
from an album dated 1847

30.17
D Tulip Designs—
St. Louis Fancy Work

Bouquets 28-35/Central Rose of Sharon 31

31.1
T Golden Rose of Virginia—
Nancy Cabot, *Chicago Tribune* 1933

31.23
T Pennsylvania Rose—
Capper's Weekly

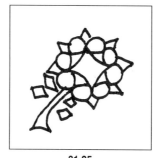

31.25
T Harrison Rose—
Nancy Cabot, *Chicago Tribune* 1933
and Mountain Mist #L

31.26
T Harrison Rose—
Hall and Kretsinger, pg. 114

31.33
T Rose Applique—
McKim/*101 Quilt Patterns*, pg. 10

31.34
T Rappahannock Rose—
Nancy Cabot, *Chicago Tribune* 1937

31.42
T Rose of Sharon—
Webster

31.44
T Rose in Bud—
from a quilt ca. 1850 in Bacon,
pg 156 Much of this block is
actually pieced

31.46
T Rosebud Patchwork Quilt—
unknown clipping ca. 1890

31.52
T Rose of Sharon—
Hall and Kretsinger, pg. 112

31.54
T Virginia Rose—
Webster

31.6
T The Rose Sprig—
Carlie Sexton/*Old Fashioned Quilts*

31.72
T Rose of Sharon—
Peto/*American Quilts*

31.73
T Rose of Sharon—
Nancy Cabot, *Chicago Tribune*

31.75
T Rose of Sharon—
McKim/*101 Quilt Patterns*, pg. 81

31.82
T Early Rose of Sharon—
Finley, plate 65

31.83
T Rose of Sharon—
Hall and Kretsinger, pg. 113

31.85
T Ohio Beauty—
quilt by Whitehill in Denver Art
Museum

31.87
T Unnamed—
from a quilt in Bishop and Coblentz,
pg. 100

31.92
T Unnamed—
from a quilt in Safford and Bishop,
pg. 184
Asymmetrical Rose—
Kimball

31.93
T American Beauty Rose—
Webster in *Ladies Home Journal*,
1911 See similar patterns
numbered 45.23

31.95
T Unnamed—
from a quilt dated 1855 in
Lasansky/*Pieced By Mother*, pg. 67

31.97
T Unnamed—
from a quilt dated 1855 in
Lasansky/*Pieced By Mother*, pg. 67

31.99
T Unknown—
from a quilt in Roberson/North
Carolina, pg. 95 The North Carolina
Project found several examples.

Bouquets/Miscellaneous 32-33

32.11
D Dogwood—
Wheeler/Brooks

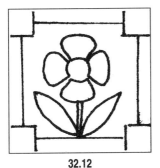

32.12
D Meadow Rose—
Nancy Cabot, *Chicago Tribune* 1936

32.13
D Dogwood—
Nancy Cabot, *Chicago Tribune* 1936

32.14
D Wild Rose—
Aunt Martha/*Prize-Winning Quilts*
Aunt Martha's Wild Rose—
Hall and Kretsinger, pg. 111

32.22
D Bowknot—
Needlecraft Magazine 1935

32.24
D Unnamed—
Needlecraft Magazine 1940

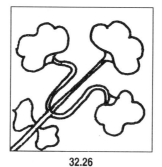

32.26
T Yellow Wildfire—
Nancy Cabot, *Chicago Tribune* 1938

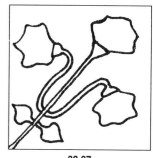

32.27
T Peony—
Elizabeth Daingerfield,
Ladies Home Journal 1912

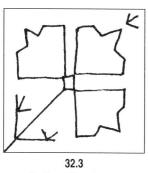

32.3
D Rose Geranium—
Nancy Cabot, *Chicago Tribune* 1935

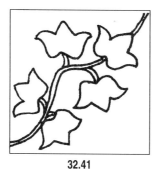

32.41
D Ivy—
Nancy Cabot, *Chicago Tribune* 1937

32.42
D Sage Brush Block—
Nancy Cabot, *Chicago Tribune* 1935

32.51
D Unnamed—
Successful Farming 6/1930

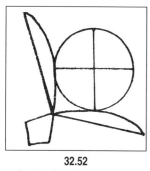

32.52
D Evening Flower Block—
Nancy Cabot, *Chicago Tribune* 1934

32.54
D Baby Chrysthanthemum—
Nancy Cabot, *Chicago Tribune* 1934

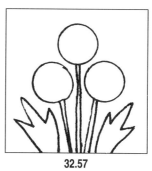

32.57
D Globe Thistle—
Nancy Cabot, *Chicago Tribune* 1934

32.58
D Marigolds—
Nancy Cabot, *Chicago Tribune* 1938

32.59
D Pompon—
Nancy Cabot, *Chicago Tribune* 1936

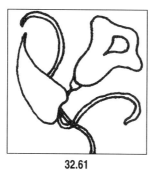

32.61
D Calla Lily—
Nancy Cabot, *Chicago Tribune* 1934

32.62
D Bluebells and Splendors—
Rainbow stamped block #720B

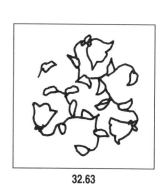

32.63
D Woodland Bells—
Rainbow stamped block #575c

32.71
T Unnamed—
from an album dated 1861

32.74
D Decorative Flowers—
Nancy Cabot, *Chicago Tribune* 1935

32.75
D Bluebell Quilt—
Wheeler/Brooks

32.76
D Lily of the Valley—
Wheeler/Brooks #1017

32.81
D Blue Bells—
Nancy Cabot, *Chicago Tribune* 1934

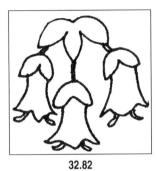

32.82
D Cathedral Bells—
Nancy Cabot, *Chicago Tribune* 1934

32.83
D Lilies of the Valley—
Nancy Cabot, *Chicago Tribune* 1935

32.84
D Bell and Flower—
Nancy Cabot, *Chicago Tribune* 1935

32.85
D Lily of the Valley—
Nancy Cabot, *Chicago Tribune*

32.87
D Wisteria—
Nancy Cabot, *Chicago Tribune* 1935

32.91
D Tree of Life—
Aunt Martha ca. 1933

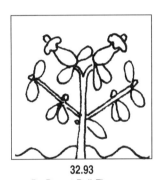

32.93
D Desert Bell Flower—
Nancy Cabot, *Chicago Tribune* 1936

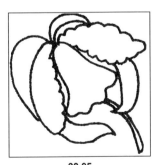

32.95
D Orchids—
Nancy Cabot, *Chicago Tribune* 1933

33.12
T The Love Rose—
Ladies Art Company #188

33.13
T Poinsettia—
Webster (alternated with #21.13)

33.15
T Cactus Flower—
Needlecraft Magazine 1935
Blooming Cactus—
Nancy Cabot, *Chicago Tribune* 1935

33.16
T Single Bud—
Nancy Cabot, *Chicago Tribune* 1938

33.18
T Heirloom Historic Quilt—
Wheeler/Brooks

33.21
T Whig Rose—
Webster, fig. 48

33.22
T Tiger Lily and Bud—
Nancy Cabot, *Chicago Tribune* 1935

33.24
T Whig Rose—
Hall and Kretsinger, pg. 114

33.25
T Lotus Flower—
Shelburne Museum

33.32
T Dixie Rose—
from a quilt ca. 1850
in *North Carolina Quilts*, pg.182

33.37
T Olive Branch—
Ladies Art Company #110
Tulip Design—
Wilkinson

33.41
D Unnamed—
Aunt Martha ca. 1933
Wild Flower—
Nancy Cabot, *Chicago Tribune* 1937

33.42
Old Dutch Tulip—
Hall and Kretsinger, pg. 122

33.43
D Canada Lily—
Nancy Cabot, *Chicago Tribune* 1933

33.44
D Rose Garden—
Nancy Cabot, *Chicago Tribune*

33.45
D Old Persia—
Nancy Cabot, *Chicago Tribune* 1937

33.46
D Flower Tree—
Grandmother Clark

33.47
D Flower Spears—
Nancy Cabot, *Chicago Tribune* 1936

33.48
D Fuschia Quilt—
Modern Priscilla 1925

33.52
D Poinsettia—
Webster design 1917

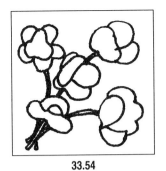

33.54
D Autumn Flowers—
Hall and Kretsinger, pg. 106

33.56
D Hollyhock—
Capper's Weekly

33.59
D Field Flowers—
Paragon

33.61
T Unnamed—
from a sampler dated 1855
in *North Carolina Quilts*

33.62
T Chrysthanthemum—
Arkansas Quilters Guild

33.63
D Chrysthanthemum—
Hearth and Home

33.64
D Mexican Shell Flower—
Nancy Cabot, *Chicago Tribune* 1934

33.72
D Salvia—
Nancy Cabot, *Chicago Tribune* 1934

33.74
D Mignonette—
Nancy Cabot, *Chicago Tribune* 1934

33.76
D Modern Flower Block—
Nancy Cabot, *Chicago Tribune* 1936

33.81
D Delphiniums—
Nancy Cabot, *Chicago Tribune*

33.83
D Cliveden Quilt—
McCall's

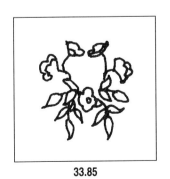

33.85
D Wayside Roses—
Webster ca. 1925

33.87
D Poinsettia—
Rainbow stamped block #841

33.9
T Shaw Family Pattern—
Whitehill in Denver Art Museum

101

34.11
D Burning Bush—
Nancy Cabot, *Chicago Tribune* 1934

34.12
D Viscaria—
Nancy Cabot, *Chicago Tribune* 1934

34.14
D Pansy Block—
Nancy Cabot, *Chicago Tribune*

34.16
D Columbine—
Nancy Cabot, *Chicago Tribune*

34.18
D Anemone—
Nancy Cabot, *Chicago Tribune* 1934

34.19
D Rose of the Field—
Needlecraft Magazine 1933

34.22
D Kentucky Columbine—
Nancy Cabot, *Chicago Tribune* 1936

34.24
D Larkspur—
Nancy Cabot, *Chicago Tribune*

34.26
D Rose of Heaven—
Nancy Cabot, *Chicago Tribune*

34.28
D Azalea—
Nancy Cabot, *Chicago Tribune* 1937

34.29
D Damask Rose—
Comfort

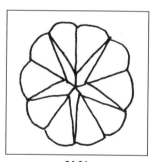

34.31
D Moonflower—
Nancy Cabot, *Chicago Tribune*

34.33
Texas Republic—
Nancy Cabot, *Chicago Tribune* 1936

34.42
D Corsage Bouquet—
Aunt Martha/*Prize-winning Quilts*
Morning Glory—
Hetty Winthrop (aka Nancy Cabot)

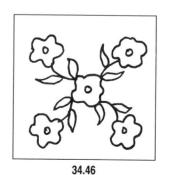

34.46
T Wild Rose Spray—
Nancy Cabot, *Chicago Tribune*
Spray with Wild Roses—
Nancy Cabot, *Chicago Tribune* 1945

34.47
T Wild Rose—
Carlie Sexton

34.48
T Modern Wild Rose—
Comfort

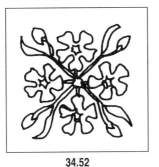

34.52
D Angel's Breath—
Nancy Cabot, *Chicago Tribune* 1934

34.54
D Wild Rose—
Ladies Art Company #447

34.56
D Jasmine—
Nancy Cabot, *Chicago Tribune* 1937

34.57
D Forget Me Not—
Nancy Cabot, *Chicago Tribune* 1938

34.58
D Unnamed—
Needlework Magazine 1923

34.59
D Snow in July—
Nancy Cabot, *Chicago Tribune* 1934

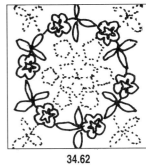

34.62
D Strawberry Block—
Nancy Cabot, *Chicago Tribune* 1938

34.64
D Wild Rose #3—
Nancy Cabot, *Chicago Tribune* 1933

34.65
D Wild Rose—
Nancy Cabot, *Chicago Tribune* 1933

34.67
D Verbena—
Rainbow stamped block

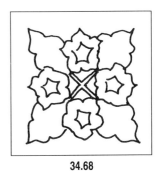

34.68
D Primrose—
Nancy Cabot, *Chicago Tribune*
Giant Primrose—
Nancy Cabot, *Chicago Tribune* 1938

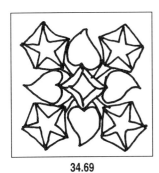

34.69
D Morning Glory—
Ladies Art Company #418, also
Mountain Mist

34.72
D Wild Rose—
Comfort

34.74
D Wildwood Wreath—
Farmer's Wife

34.75
D Dogwood Flower—
Rainbow stamped block #177c

35.12
D Forget Me Not—
Mountain Mist #61

35.13
D Unnamed—
Needlecraft Magazine 1923

35.14
D Rose Spray—
Nancy Cabot, *Chicago Tribune* 1934

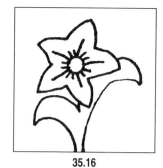

35.16
D Blue Petunia—
Nancy Cabot, *Chicago Tribune* 1938

35.17
D Rose Garden—
Nancy Cabot, *Chicago Tribune*

35.22
D Lily Applique—
Wheeler/Brooks #1721

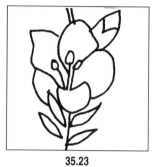

35.23
D Golden Lily—
Nancy Cabot, *Chicago Tribune* 1933

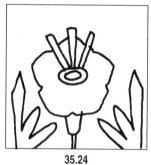

35.24
D Cardinal Climber—
Nancy Cabot, *Chicago Tribune* 1934

35.25
D Hibiscus—
Nancy Cabot, *Chicago Tribune* 1933

35.27
D Hibiscus—
Nancy Cabot, *Chicago Tribune* 1934

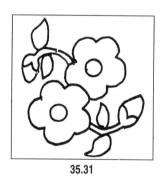

35.31
D Flower Spray—
Nancy Cabot, *Chicago Tribune* 1935

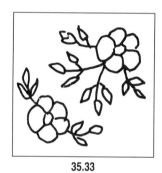

35.33
D Baby Rose—
Nancy Cabot, *Chicago Tribune* 1933

35.34
D Unnamed—
Rainbow stamped block #315

35.35
D Super Gorgeous Apple
Blossom—
Rainbow stamped block #930

35.36
D Wild Rose of the Andes—
Rainbow stamped block #736e

35.37
D Wild Rose—
Nancy Cabot, *Chicago Tribune*

104

Bouquets/Five Elements or Five-Lobed Flowers 34 & 35

35.41
D Blue Trumpet Flower—
Nancy Cabot, *Chicago Tribune* 1937

35.43
D Wild Rose Bouquet—
Nancy Cabot, *Chicago Tribune*

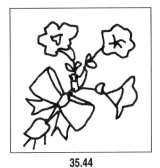

35.44
D Scattered Morning Glories—
McCall's Needlework Winter,
1941–42

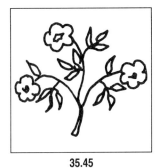

35.45
D Wisconsin Rose—
Nancy Cabot, *Chicago Tribune* 1933

35.46
D Hollyhock—
Wheeler/Brooks #403

35.47
D Source not found

35.49
D Marvel of Peru—
Rainbow stamped block #755d

35.5
D Irish Shamrock—
Rainbow stamped block #850d

35.6
D Prairie Pinks—
Nancy Cabot, *Chicago Tribune*

35.7
D Petunias—
Rainbow stamped block #854d

35.8
D Boutonnier—
Nancy Cabot, *Chicago Tribune* 1935

35.9
D Unnamed—
Rainbow stamped block #458

Six petals or Six Elements 36

36.11
A Dainty Block—
Ladies Home Journal 1896

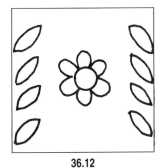

36.12
D Willow Squares—
Nancy Cabot, *Chicago Tribune* 1936

36.14
D Narcissus—
Nancy Cabot, *Chicago Tribune* 1936

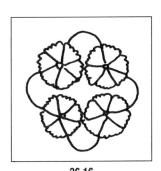

36.16
D Nasturtium—
Nancy Cabot, *Chicago Tribune* 1935

36.18
D Priscilla Alden—
Nancy Cabot, *Chicago Tribune* 1934

36.22
Tulip Wheel—
Marston and Cunningham

36.24
T Unnamed—
Aunt Martha/*Prize-winning Quilts*

36.25
T Emporia Rose—
Comfort

36.26
D Berkshire Beauty—
Nancy Cabot, *Chicago Tribune* 1937

36.32
Pennsylvania Good Luck Block—
Peto/*American Quilts*

36.33
T Mexican Rose—
Nancy Cabot, *Chicago Tribune* 1936

36.35
T Wild Rose—
Hall and Kretsinger, pg. 116

36.38
T Geometrical Rose—
Shelburne

36.43
D Solar System—
Nancy Cabot, *Chicago Tribune*

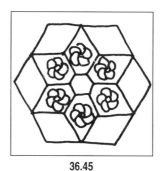

36.45
D Solomon's Garden—
Nancy Cabot, *Chicago Tribune*

36.51
D Zinnia Bouquet—
Nancy Cabot, *Chicago Tribune* 1934

36.52
D Wreath of Violets—
Nancy Cabot, *Chicago Tribune* 1934
Violet Wreath—
Nancy Cabot, *Chicago Tribune* 1937

36.53
D Sweet William—
Nancy Cabot, *Chicago Tribune* 1934

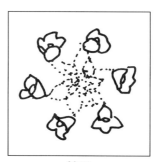

36.55
D Circle of Godetias—
Rainbow stamped block

36.56
T Cupid's Block—
Ladies Art Company #500

106

36.57
D Morning Glory—
Nancy Cabot, *Chicago Tribune* 1935

36.58
D Dianthus—
Nancy Cabot, *Chicago Tribune* 1934

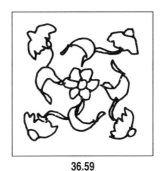

36.59
D Cornflower—
Rainbow stamped block #830

36.61
D Snowflake—
Ladies Art Company #495
Snow Crystals—
Nancy Cabot, *Chicago Tribune*

36.62
D Snowflake--
Wheeler/Brooks #7236

36.63
D Christmas Rose—
Farm Journal 1938

36.65
D Snowflake—
Ladies Home Journal 1911

36.69
D Star and Epaulettes—
Nancy Cabot, *Chicago Tribune* 1936

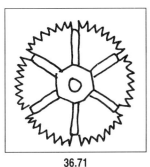

36.71
T Samoan Poppy—
Nancy Cabot, *Chicago Tribune* 1935

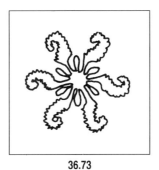

36.72
T October Foliage—
Nancy Cabot, *Chicago Tribune* 1936

36.73
T Esther's Plume—
Mrs. Danner
Indian Princess Feather—
Mrs. Danner

36.74
T Princess Feather—
Safford and Bishop, fig. 286

36.75
T Feather Rose—
Mrs. Danner

36.76
T California Plume—
Hall and Kretsinger, pg. 202

36.77
T Princess Feather—
Aunt Martha ca. 1933

36.81
D Old Fashioned Bouquet—
Nancy Cabot, *Chicago Tribune* 1934

Six Petals or Six Elements 36

36.82
T French Rose—
Aunt Martha

36.83
T Moss Ross—
Nancy Cabot, *Chicago Tribune* 1937

36.84
T Rose of Sharon—
Ladies Art Company #6056

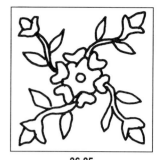

36.85
D Wind Blown Rose—
Hall and Kretsinger, pg. 109

36.86
T Tallula Rose—
Nancy Cabot, *Chicago Tribune* 1937

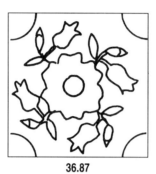

36.87
D Petunia and Bluebell—
Nancy Cabot, *Chicago Tribune*
Bluebells and Petunia—
Nancy Cabot, *Chicago Tribune*

36.88
D Unnamed—
McCall's

36.89
T Meadow Rose—
Nancy Cabot, *Chicago Tribune* 1936

Seven Petals

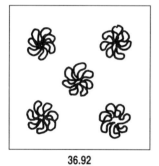

36.92
D Snowdrop Quilt—
St. Louis Fancy Work

36.94
D Snowdrop Quilt—
St. Louis Fancy Work
(these two alternate)

36.97
D Rose and Sunflowers—
Nancy Cabot, *Chicago Tribune* 1934

**Bouquets/
Stars and Roses 37.1–37.2**

37.11
T Maple Leaf—
Farmer's Wife 1932

37.12
T Double Tulip—
The Family 1913 (see variations of
these triple stars filed as pieced
designs #767-774)

37.13
T Tree of Life—
Comfort

37.14
T North Carolina Lily—
from a quilt ca. 1845

37.15
T Unnamed—
Modern Priscilla 3/1926

37.17
T   Red Peony—
Nancy Cabot, *Chicago Tribune* 1933
Flowering Balsam—
Nancy Cabot, *Chicago Tribune* 1938

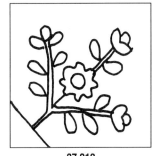

37.211
D   Dahlia—
Ladies Art Company #6005

37.212
T   Peonies—
Hall and Kretsinger, pg. 111

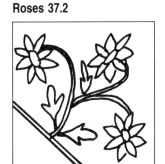

37.213
T   Kentucky Peony—
Nancy Cabot, *Chicago Tribune* 1933

37.214
T   Rose of Sharon—
from a quilt ca. 1880 in
Ramsey/*Tennessee*, pg. 42

37.215
T   Original Rose—
Webster, plate 51

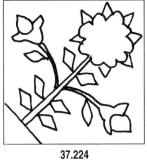

37.224
T   Rose of Sharon—
Hall and Kretsinger, pg. 111

37.226
T   Rose Tree—
McKim

37.232
D   Rose and Primrose—
Nancy Cabot, *Chicago Tribune* 1934
Rose and Daisy—
Nancy Cabot, *Chicago Tribune* 1934

37.234
T   Unnamed—
from an album dated 1854

37.236
T   Unnamed—
from an album dated 1861

37.238
T   Unnamed—
from an album dated 1861

37.144
T   Unnamed—
from an album dated 1859

37.246
D   Rose Tree—
from the border of a quilt designed
by Mountain Mist

37.25
T   Unnamed—
this rose is typical of many
elaborate blocks in Baltimore
Album quilts

37.261
D   Super Gorgeous
American Rose—
Rainbow stamped block #91

37.262
D Rose Petals—
Nancy Cabot, *Chicago Tribune*

37.263
D Unnamed—
Needlecraft Magazine 1929

37.264
D Rose Beauty—
Nancy Cabot, *Chicago Tribune* 1933

37.27
T Old Fashioned Flower Garden—
Hall and Kretsinger, pg. 106

37.28
D Rose Spray—
Comfort

37.293
T Moss Rose—
Hall and Kretsinger, pg. 170

37.294
T Four Square Rose—
MacDowell, Michigan Quilts, pg. 24

37.298
T Unnamed—
from a quilt ca. 1850
Prudence Penny

Bouquets/Water Lilies 37.3

37.31
D Magnolia Applique—
Wheeler/Brooks

37.311
D Water Lilies—
Mountain Mist

37.313
D Lotus Blossom—
Nancy Cabot, *Chicago Tribune* 1933

37.32
D Water Lilies—
Grandmother Clark

37.33
D Water Lily—
Nancy Cabot, *Chicago Tribune* 1934

37.34
D Lily Pond—
Ladies Art Company #4020
Water Lily—
Hall and Kretsinger

37.35
D Flower of Spring—
Kansas City Star 1936
(see pieced #799)

37.36
D Lily Design—
Comfort

Bouquets/Waterlilies 37.3

37.372
D Water Lily—
Rainbow stamped block #718c

37.373
D Water Lily—
Rainbow stamped block #718c

37.38
D Water Lily Circle—
Rainbow stamped block #800

37.39
D Unnamed—
Rainbow stamped block #727

Bouquets/Morning Glories 37.4

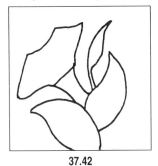

37.42
D Morning Glory—
Nancy Cabot, *Chicago Tribune* 1934
Giant Morning Glory—
Nancy Cabot, *Chicago Tribune* 1937

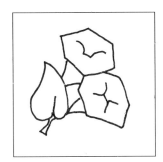

37.43
D Morning Glory—
Wheeler/Brooks

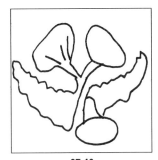

37.46
D Morning Glory—
St. Louis Fancy Work

37.49
D Morning Glories in a Circle—
Rainbow stamped block #805

Bouquets/Poppies 37.5

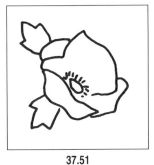

37.51
D Poppy Applique—
Wheeler/Brooks

37.52
D Flanders Poppy—
Nancy Cabot, *Chicago Tribune* 1934

37.544
D Poppy Field—
Aunt Martha
(alternates with a Red Cross)

37.546
D Poppy Garden—
Nancy Cabot, *Chicago Tribune* 1933
(alternates with #37.548)

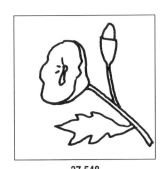

37.548
D Poppy Garden—
Nancy Cabot, *Chicago Tribune* 1933
(alternates with #37.546)

37.551
D Poppies—
Nancy Cabot, *Chicago Tribune* 1933

37.553
D Red Poppies—
Nancy Cabot, *Chicago Tribune*

37.555
D Poppy—
St. Louis Fancy Work

Bouquets/Poppies 37.5

37.56
D Poppies—
Rainbow stamped block #710

37.57
D Priscilla's Poppies—
Nancy Cabot, *Chicago Tribune* 1935

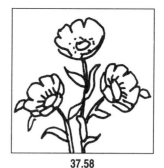

37.58
D Poppies—
Rainbow stamped block #320

37.59
D Field Flowers—
Nancy Cabot, *Chicago Tribune* 1934

Bouquets/Pansies 37.6

37.61
D Pansy—
Sears 1934

37.62
D Pansy Applique—
Wheeler/Brooks

37.63
D Pansy—
Star and Pansy Design—
Ladies Art Company

37.64
D Pansy—
Wheeler/Brooks

37.65
D Gay Print Pansy—
Needlecraft Magazine

37.662
D Pansies—
Rainbow stamped block #535s

37.664
D Gorgeous Pansies—
Rainbow stamped block #838

37.665
D Pansies—
Rainbow stamped block #300

Bouquets/Iris 37.7

37.67
D Pansies—
Wheeler/Brooks #7044

37.68
D Pansy Block—
Nancy Cabot, *Chicago Tribune* 1933

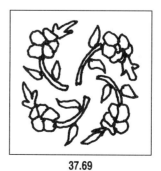

37.69
D Pansy Design—
Ladies Art Company #6065

37.7
D Flags—
Rainbow stamped block #712

Bouquets/Iris 37.7

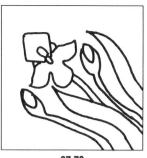

37.72
D Iris Applique—
McKim #369

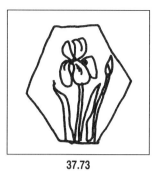

37.73
D Unnamed—
Aunt Martha

37.742
D Iris—
Mountain Mist

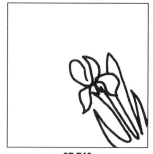

37.743
D Iris—
Boag kit

37.75
D Iris—
Ladies Art Company #6085

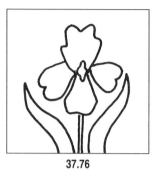

37.76
D Purple Iris—
Nancy Cabot, *Chicago Tribune* 1934

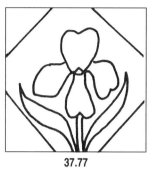

37.77
D Simple Iris—
Nancy Cabot, *Chicago Tribune* 1935

37.78
D Conventional Fleur-de-Lis—
Comfort
Tiger Lily—
Comfort

Bouquets/Daffodils 37.8

37.79
Iris—
Nancy Cabot, *Chicago Tribune* 1933

37.81
D Narcissus—
Wheeler/Brooks

37.82
D Daffodils—
Nancy Cabot, *Chicago Tribune*

37.84
D Daffodils—
Aunt Martha

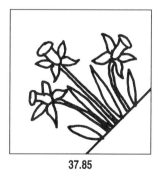

37.85
D Jonquils—
Nancy Cabot, *Chicago Tribune* 1936

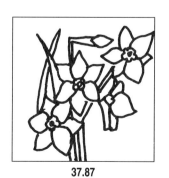

37.87
D Narcissus—
Nancy Cabot, *Chicago Tribune* 1933

37.88
D Rainbow Quilt—
Webster

37.89
D Dancing Daffodil—
Home Art

37.913
D Conventional Flower—
Hearth and Home

37.915
D Friendship Dahlia—
Hall and Kretsinger, pg. 104

37.917
D Kansas Sunflower—
Capper's Weekly 1930

37.923
D Poinsettia—
Hall and Kretsinger, pg. 106

37.924
D Modern Poinsettia—
Nancy Cabot, *Chicago Tribune*

37.926
D Brown-Eyed Susans—
Nancy Cabot, *Chicago Tribune* 1933

37.932
Sunflower—
Nancy Cabot, *Chicago Tribune* 1936

37.934
T Old Sunflower—
Nancy Cabot, *Chicago Tribune* 1937

37.936
T Southern Sunflower—
Hearth and Home

37.94
T Unnamed—
from a quilt 1860–1885
Spencer Museum of Art

37.95
T Unnamed—
from a mid-nineteenth century quilt
in the *Quilt Engagement Calendar*
1979, pg. 23

37.96
Zinnia Border—
Mountain Mist

37.97
T Sunflower—
from a quilt ca. 1861 Vermont

37.981
D Blanket Flower—
Nancy Cabot, *Chicago Tribune* 1934

37.982
D Sun God—
Nancy Cabot, *Chicago Tribune*

37.99
D Feather Flower—
Nancy Cabot, *Chicago Tribune* 1934

38.1
T Unnamed—
from an album dated 1848

38.22
D Horn of Plenty—
Ladies Art Company

38.23
D Horn of Plenty—
Needlecraft Magazine

38.24
D Horn of Penty—
Nancy Cabot, *Chicago Tribune* 1933

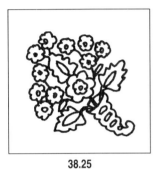

38.25
D Ladies Art Company #6082

38.32
D Horn of Plenty—
Nancy Cabot, *Chicago Tribune*

38.34
D Horn of Plenty—
Paragon kit
Garden Bounty—
Wheeler/Brooks #662

38.4
D Horn of Plenty—
Hall and Kretsinger

38.52
T Unnamed—
from an album dated 1848. These
striped cornucopia are typical of
Baltimore Album quilts

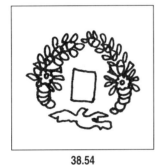

38.54
T Unnamed—
from an album dated 1847

38.55
T Unnamed—
from an album dated 1840 (this
date seems a few years too early)

38.6
T Unnamed—
from a cut-out chintz quilt ca. 1830
in the Shelburne Museum #29

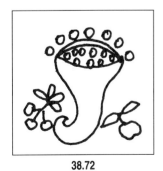

38.72
T Unnamed—
from an album dated 1861

38.76
T Unnamed—
from an album dated 1861

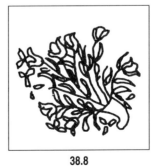

38.8
T Unnamed—
from a quilt dated 1814 in the
Shelburne Museum #140

38.9
T Unnamed—
from an album dated 1860

39.13
D A Charming Nosegay—
McKim
Old Fashioned Nosegay—
Hall and Kretsinger, pg. 106

39.15
D Nosegay—
Needlecraft Magazine 1933

39.24
D English Flower Garden—McKim
English Garden—*Capper's Weekly*
Old English Flower Garden—
Kansas City Star

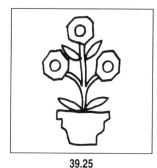

39.25
D Dutch Roses—
Nancy Cabot, *Chicago Tribune* 1935

39.34
D Geranium—
Aunt Martha

39.36
D Magyar Flower Pot—
Nancy Cabot, *Chicago Tribune*

39.43
D Rose Flower Pot—
Mrs. Danner

39.45
D Pot of Tulips—
Nancy Cabot, *Chicago Tribune* 1933

39.46
D Unnamed—
Needlecraft Magazine 5/1923

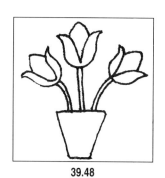

39.48
D Tulip in a Pot—
Carlie Sexton
Cut Tulips—
Nancy Cabot, *Chicago Tribune* 1934

39.51
D Petunia—
Nancy Cabot, *Chicago Tribune* 1934

39.52
D Pot of Flowers—
Grandmother Clark Book 21, 1931

39.53
D Pot of Flowers—
Nancy Cabot, *Chicago Tribune* 1935

39.55
D Grandmother's Prize Quilt—
Wheeler/Brooks

39.57
D Sweetheart Rose—
Needlecraft Magazine

39.59
D Dahlia Flower Pot—
Nancy Cabot, *Chicago Tribune* 1937

39.6
D Phillipsburg (PA) Flower Pot—
Nancy Cabot, *Chicago Tribune* 1936

39.7
D Daffodil—
Herschnner (see as a series)

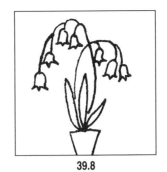

39.8
D Bluebell Block—
Nancy Cabot, *Chicago Tribune* 1936

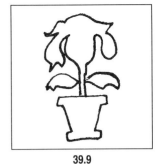

39.9
D Gingham Bush—
Nancy Cabot, *Chicago Tribune* 1935

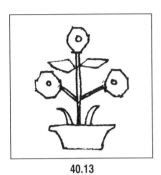

40.13
D Flowers in a Pot—
Ickis pg. 44

40.15
D Pot of Poppies—
Nancy Cabot, *Chicago Tribune*

40.22
D Box of Tulips—
Kansas City Star 3/7/1951

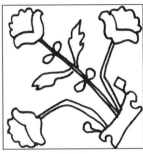

40.24
T Tulip Pot—
Marston and Cunningham

40.32
T Unnamed—
Modern Priscilla

40.35
D Yellow Iris—
Nancy Cabot, *Chicago Tribune* 1934

40.36
D Box of Pansies—
Nancy Cabot, *Chicago Tribune* 1933

40.38
D Unnamed—
Needlecraft Magazine 1923

40.41
T Sahara Rose—
Nancy Cabot, *Chicago Tribune* 1936

40.42
T Unnamed—
Webster, fig. 35

40.45
D Unnamed—
Successful Farming 6/1930

40.47
T Unnamed—
from an album dated 1865

40.5
Flower Urn—
Aunt Martha/*Prize-winning Quilts*

40.63
T Tulip—
Source not found

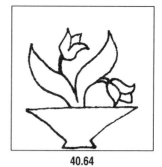

40.64
D Unnamed—
Aunt Martha/*Prize-winning Quilts*

40.66
D Unnamed—
Aunt Martha/*Prize-winning Quilts*

40.7
D Tulip Bowl—
Mountain Mist

40.9
D Source not found

41.12
T Coxcomb—
Nancy Cabot, *Chicago Tribune*

41.13
D Basket of Spring—
Rainbow
Flower of Spring—
Needlecraft Magazine 1923

41.16
T Flower Basket—
Hall and Kretsinger, pg. 186

41.19
T Lotus Blossom—
Bresenhan/Texas

41.2
D Tile Flower—
Aunt Martha ca. 1933

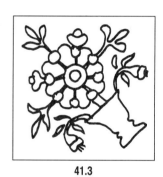

41.3
T Seth Thomas Rose—
Kansas City Star 1929

41.42
T Coxcomb—
Shelburne

41.44
T Coxcomb—
Bishop and Coblentz

41.46
T Cockscomb—
Finley, plate 77

41.48
T Coxcomb—
Hall and Kretsinger, pg. 120

41.49
T Cactus Rose—
Bishop and Coblentz, pg. 74

41.51
T Unnamed—
Bishop and Coblentz, pg. 70

41.52
T Unnamed—
from a quilt in *Quilt Engagment Calendar* 1982, plate 32

41.53
T Unnamed—
from a quilt ca. 1870 *Quilter's Newsletter* 4/1992

41.54
T Flower Urn—
from a quilt ca. 1880
by Susan McCord in Greenfield Village

41.551
T Potted Tulip—
Farm and Fireside 9/1929

41.552
T Pride of Iowa—
Hall and Kretsinger, pg. 242
Four Little Birds —
Shelburne (has 2 more birds)

41.56
T Egyptian Lotus Flower—
Hall and Kretsinger, pg. 198

41.6
T Unnamed—
Prudence Penny

41.72
T Urn—
Hall and Kretsinger, pg. 120

41.74
T Peony—
from a quilt by Whitehill in the Denver Art Museum

41.8
T Unnamed—
Bresenhan/Texas

41.91
Rose—
Farmer's Wife 1932

41.93
Decorative Plant—
Nancy Cabot, *Chicago Tribune* 1935

41.95
D Rose Basket—
Rural New Yorker 1934

41.97
T Vase of Roses—
Sienkiewicz

41.99
T Democratic Rose—
Nancy Cabot, *Chicago Tribune* 1935

42.1
T Tulip Design—
Kansas City Star 2/5/1932

42.23
D Unnamed—
Needlecraft Magazine 1940

42.24
D Jonquils—
Nancy Cabot, *Chicago Tribune* 1933

42.25
D Nasturtiums—
Nancy Cabot, *Chicago Tribune* 1933

42.26
D Breath of Springtime—
Nancy Cabot, *Chicago Tribune* 1933

42.35
D Garden Bouquet—
Nancy Page (see as a series)

42.37
D Fragrance—
Nancy Cabot, *Chicago Tribune* 1933

42.41
T Cactus Rose—
Finley, pg. 66

42.43
T Unnamed—
from a quilt ca. 1870 in
Quilt Digest 1985

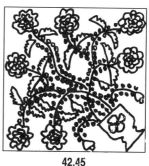

42.45
T Unnamed—
from a quilt dated 1886, collection:
A.Savage

42.46
T Unnamed—
from an album dated 1855

42.47
T Unnamed—
from an album dated 1848

42.48
T Unnamed—
from an album dated 1859

42.53
T Unnamed—
Prudence Penny

42.54
T French Provincial—
Nancy Cabot, *Chicago Tribune* 1935

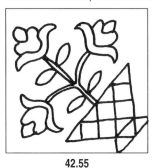

42.55
T Lily Basket—
Nancy Cabot, *Chicago Tribune* 1936

42.56
T Basket of Flowers—
Nancy Cabot, *Chicago Tribune* 1935

42.58
Tulip Basket—
Nancy Cabot, *Chicago Tribune* 1933

42.61
T Unnamed—
Modern Priscilla

42.623
T Unnamed—
from an album ca. 1850

42.625
T Unnamed—
Modern Priscilla 3/1926

42.634
D Wild Rose—
Ladies Art Company

42.635
D Rose Basket—
Nancy Cabot, *Chicago Tribune*

42.642
T Potted Rose—
Nancy Cabot, *Chicago Tribune* 1938

42.643
T Rose and Dahlia—
Nancy Cabot, *Chicago Tribune*

42.65
D Bleeding Hearts—
Sears 1934

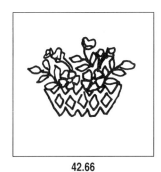

42.66
D Flower Basket—
Webster in *Ladies Home Journal*
8/1911

42.67
T Unnamed—
from an album dated 1855

42.68
T Unnamed—
from an album dated 1853

42.692
T Rustic Basket—
inscribed on an album dated 1849

42.694
T Swiss Basket—
inscribed on an album dated 1840
These graceful wicker baskets are
typical of blocks in elaborate
Baltimore Album quilts

42.713
Decorated Basket—
Nancy Cabot, *Chicago Tribune* 1934

42.715
Flower Basket—
Carlie Sexton
Carlie Sexton's Basket—
Hall and Kretsinger, pg. 126

42.717
D Mrs. Halls Basket—
Hall and Kretsinger, pg. 126

42.72
D May Basket—
Kansas City Star 1946

42.732
D Flower Basket—
Ladies Art Company

42.733
D Basket of Daisies—
Hall and Kretsinger, pg. 126

42.735
D Flower Basket—
Nancy Cabot, *Chicago Tribune* 1933

42.742
D Flower Basket—
Nancy Cabot, *Chicago Tribune* 1935

42.743
D May Basket—
Needlecraft Magazine 1933

42.745
D Maude Hare's Basket—
Hall and Kretsinger, pg. 126

42.746
D Basket—
Farmer's Wife 1932

42.752
D French Basket—
Webster (alternates with scroll block)
Ivory Basket—
Mrs. Danner

42.754
D Basket Applique—
Kansas City Star 1935

42.756
D Unnamed—
Needlecraft 1923

42.76
D Basket of Roses—
Nancy Cabot, *Chicago Tribune* 1933

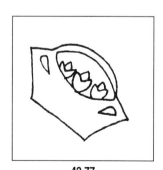

42.77
D Dutch Tulip Basket—
Nancy Cabot, *Chicago Tribune* 1933

122

42.78
D Garden Gift—
Needlecraft Magazine 2/1935 pg. 9

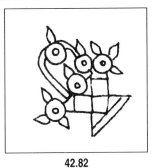

42.82
D Unnamed—
Aunt Martha ca. 1933

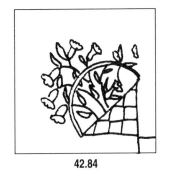

42.84
D Bells in Bloom—
Nancy Cabot, *Chicago Tribune* 1933

42.85
D Golden Poppies—
Nancy Cabot, *Chicago Tribune* 1933

42.91
D Iris in Baskets—
Webster

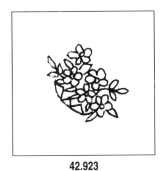

42.923
D Unnamed—
Aunt Martha ca. 1933

42.924
Bowl of Flowers—
Nancy Cabot, *Chicago Tribune* 1933

42.93
D Egyptian Lotus—
Nancy Cabot, *Chicago Tribune* 1935

42.94
D Blue Basket—
Paragon kit

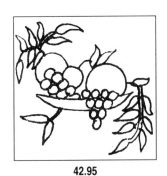

42.95
D Fruit Bowl—
Nancy Cabot, *Chicago Tribune* 1935

42.96
D Vase of Posies—
Capper's Weekly ca. 1925

42.97
D Vase of Roses—
Nancy Cabot, *Chicago Tribune* 1934

42.992
D Tulip Garden—
Ladies Art Company #6071

42.993
D Tulip Garden—
Nancy Cabot, *Chicago Tribune* 1933

42.995
D Hearts and Flowers—
Nancy Cabot, *Chicago Tribune* 1934

42.997
D Wax Flowers—
Nancy Cabot, *Chicago Tribune* 1937

43.12
Unnamed—
Ladies Art Company #878

43.14
Four Leaf Clover—
Kansas City Star 1947

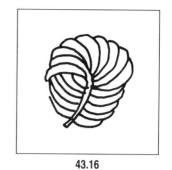

43.16
Yellow Plume—
Nancy Cabot, *Chicago Tribune* 1936

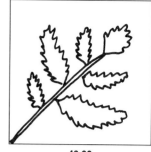

43.22
T Oak Leaf—
Rural New Yorker

43.24
T Hop Vine—
name inscribed on a quilt ca. 1870
Shelburne

43.26
T Unnamed—
from an album dated 1857

43.28
T Ameranth—
from a quilt dated 1858 Indiana

43.33
T Trailing Vines—
Nancy Cabot, *Chicago Tribune* 1936

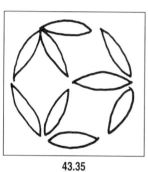

43.35
D Autumn Leaves—
Nancy Cabot, *Chicago Tribune* 1935

43.42
T Unnamed—
from an album dated 1851

43.43
T True Lover's Knot—
name inscribed on a quilt ca. 1870
Shelburne

43.45
T Unnamed—
from an album dated 1846

43.48
T Pride of the Forest—
Finley

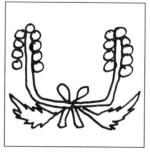

43.52
T Poke Berries—
name inscribed on a quilt ca. 1870
Shelburne #10.323

43.54
T Cherries—
Nancy Cabot, *Chicago Tribune* 1933

43.55
T Unnamed—
from an album dated 1848

43.62
T Unnamed—
from an album dated 1852

43.64
T Unnamed—
from an album dated 1856

43.65
T Unnamed—
from an album dated 1847

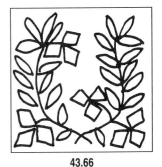

43.66
T Unnamed—
from an album dated 1857

43.72
T Cockscomb Variation—
from a quilt in *Quilt Engagement Calendar* 1984, plate 31

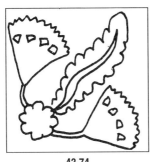

43.74
T The Olive Branch—
Ladies Home Journal 1908

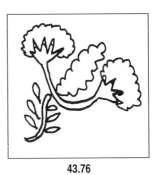

43.76
T Coxcomb—
Bishop and Coblentz

43.78
T Unnamed—
from a quilt ca. 1870 in
Quilt Engagement Calendar 1988,
plate 25

43.82
T Tree of Life—
Bresenhan/Texas

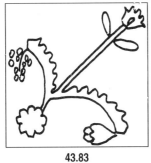

43.83
T Tulip Pattern—
Vickery Publishing

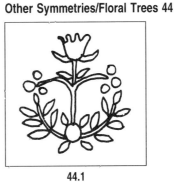

44.1
T Prairie Rose—
Rural New Yorker

44.2
T Tulip Design—
Ickis pg. 112

44.3
T Tulip Tree—
from a quilt ca. 1850
Spencer Museum

44.4
T Conventional Tulip—
Ickis, pg. 19

44.5
T Rose and Buds—
Nancy Cabot, *Chicago Tribune* 1937

44.6
T Prairie Flower—
Carlie Sexton

125

44.7

T Prairie Flower—
Hall and Kretsinger
Missouri Rose—
Hall and Kretsinger
Rose Tree—
Hall and Kretsinger

44.8

T Rambling Rose—
Bresenhan/Texas

44.9

T Unnamed—
from a quilt dated 1869,
Kansas Quilt Project

45.12

T Unnamed—
from a quilt ca. 1860

45.14

D Blue and White Quilt—
Ladies Home Journal 1908

45.16

D Sunlight and Shadows—
Nancy Cabot, *Chicago Tribune* 1936

45.18

D Tulip Garden—
Nancy Cabot, *Chicago Tribune* 1935

45.19

D Conventional Tulip—
Farmer's Wife 10/1929

45.23

D Pink Rose—
Webster (see also 31.93)
Rose with Watermelon Border—
Mrs. Danner

45.24

D Rose of Sharon—
Ladies Art Company #44

45.26

T Kentucky Rose—
Ladies Art Company #42

45.28

T Rose of LeMoyne—
Nancy Cabot, *Chicago Tribune* 1935

45.32

Sweet Pea—
Nancy Cabot, *Chicago Tribune* 1934

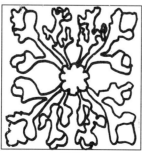

45.34

T The Poppy—
Finley, pg. 65

45.36

T Unnamed—
Comfort

45.38

T Unnamed—
from an album dated 1844

126

45.42
T   True Lover's Knot—
Omaha World Herald 1912
Conventional Scroll—
Nancy Cabot, *Chicago Tribune*
A Kansas Pattern—
Whitehill in Denver Art Museum

45.44
T   Unnamed—
from an album dated 1847

45.5
T   Unnamed—
from an album dated 1847

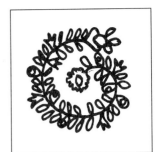

45.6
T   Unnamed—
from an album dated 1847

45.72
T   Persian Palm Lily—
Ladies Art Company #52

45.74
T   Unnamed—
from an album dated 1860

45.79
Hunter's Horn—
Hearth and Home

45.81
T   Unnamed—
from an album dated 1845

45.82
D   Gay Garden—
Webster ca. 1925

45.83
T   Unnamed—
from an album dated 1844

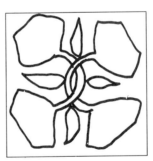

45.85
D   Jerusalem Cross—
Nancy Cabot, *Chicago Tribune* 1934

45.86
T   Rose of LeMoyne—
Nancy Cabot, *Chicago Tribune* 1933

45.87
T   Old Fashioned Rose—
Hall and Kretsinger pg. 111

45.88
T   Unnamed—
from an album dated 1863

45.92
T   Unnamed—
from an album dated 1854

45.94
D   Swedona Block—
Nancy Cabot, *Chicago Tribune* 1938

46.12
D Adam and Eve—
Nancy Cabot, *Chicago Tribune* 1934
Garden of Eden—
Nancy Cabot, *Chicago Tribune* 1937

46.14
D Peaches—
Nancy Cabot, *Chicago Tribune* 1934

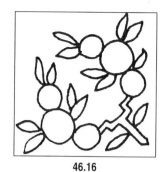

46.16
D Maude Hare's Flower Garden—
Hall and Kretsinger, pg. 107

46.22
D Autumn Fruit—
Farm Journal 1936

46.24
D Victory Garden—
Wheeler/Brooks #7516

46.31
T Strawberry—
Hall and Kretsinger

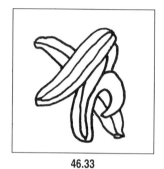

46.33
D Banana—
block from the Horn of Plenty series
#73.8

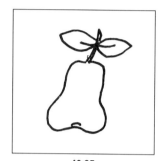

46.35
D Pear—
block from the Garden Fruit series
#73.9

46.41
T Pineapple Design—
Webster, fig. 52
Modern Pineapple—
Mrs. Danner

46.42
T The Pineapple—
Needlecraft Magazine May, 1928

46.44
T Pineapple—
Nancy Cabot, *Chicago Tribune* 1933

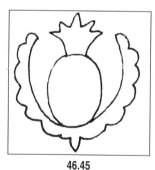

46.45
T Pineapple—
Ickis, pg. 82

46.46
T Unnamed—
from a quilt in the *Quilt
Engagement Calendar* 1978, plate
56

46.47
T Pieced Pineapple—
Finley plate 80

46.48
T Unnamed—
from a quilt in Lasansky,
Pieced by Mother, pg. 56

46.49
T Unnamed—
from an album dated 1860

46.61
T Love Apple—
Finley and Carlie Sexton

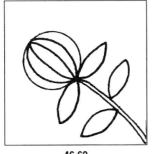

46.62
T Love Apple—
Hall and Kretsinger pg. 106

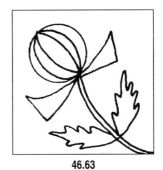

46.63
T Love Apple—
Nancy Cabot, *Chicago Tribune* 1933

46.64
T Love Apple—
McKim

46.65
T California Rose—
Aunt Martha

46.66
T Rose of LeMoyne—
Hall and Kretsinger, pg. 114

46.68
T Unnamed—
Ladies Circle Patchwork Quilts,
Spring 1984

46.69
T The Peach—
Comfort

46.72
T Temperance Ball—
Carlie Sexton, Old Fashioned Quilts

46.74
T Pomegranate—
Mountain Mist

46.76
T Unnamed—
Safford and Bishop, pg. 188

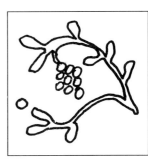

46.81
T Unnamed—
from an album dated 1847

46.83
T Grapes—
Nancy Cabot, *Chicago Tribune* 1934

46.86
T Wild Grape—
Comfort

46.88
T Unnamed—
Lasansky, *Pennsylvania Papers*

46.89
T Wild Cherries—
Hearth and Home

129

47.11
D Sunbonnet Baby—
Quilt World February, 1977

47.12
D Sunbonnet Sue—
Mrs. Danner

47.13
D Sunbonnet Susie—
Nancy Cabot, *Chicago Tribune* 1940

47.14
D Sunbonnet Baby—
Nancy Cabot, *Chicago Tribune*

47.15
D Sunbonnet Sue—
Ladies Art Company 1900–1925

47.16
D Sunbonnet Baby—
Rainbow 1932

47.17
D Little Dutch Girl—
Frank's

47.22
D Sunbonnet Sue—
Eveline Foland in
Kansas City Star 1930

47.24
D Mary Ann—
Nancy Cabot, *Chicago Tribune* 1933

47.26
D Mary Lou—
Nancy Cabot, *Chicago Tribune*

47.28
D Remember—
Eveline Johnson,
Needlecraft Magazine 1936

47.32
D Unnamed—
Ordell, early 20th century

47.33
D Flower Girl—
Sears, Roebuck and Co., 1934
(alternates with #53.44)

47.37
D Sunbonnet Girl—
Workbasket, April, 1977

47.42
D Sunbonnet Sue—
Jinny Beyer in *Quilter's Newsletter
Magazine* March, 1975

47.44
D Unnamed—
unknown clipping

47.48
D Dutch Girl—
Nancy Cabot, *Chicago Tribune* 1933

47.52
D Calico Girls—
Nancy Cabot, *Chicago Tribune*
(Cabot had many variations
of this figure)

47.54
D Old Fashioned Lady—
Aunt Martha

47.56
D Bride Quilt—
Aunt Martha

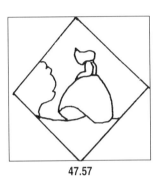

47.57
D Old Fashioned Girl—
Wheeler/Brooks #798

47.58
D Colonial Ladies—
Vogue

47.61
D Unnamed—
Needlecraft Magazine 1932

47.63
D Unnamed—
Sears, Roebuck and Co., 1934

47.65
D Unnamed—
Rainbow

47.67
D Sunbonnet Girls Running
Between the Raindrops—
Wheeler/Brooks #7144

47.72
D Balloon Girl—
Wheeler/Brooks #709

47.74
D Balloon Girl—
Wheeler/Brooks

47.82
D Sunbonnet Girl—
Wheeler/Brooks #7337

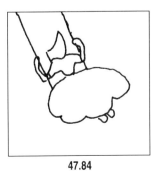

47.84
D Old Fashioned Girl in a Swing—
Wheeler/Brooks #723

47.86
D Sunbonnet Sue—
Wheeler/Brooks #5025A

47.9
D Colonial Lady—
Grandma Dexter.
See as a series #74.21

48.12
D Overall Bill—
Ladies Art Company 1900–1925

48.13
D Overall Boy—
Frank's

48.16
D Straw Hat Boy—
Mrs. Danner

48.17
D Dutch Boy—
Nancy Cabot, *Chicago Tribune* 1942

48.22
D Sunny Jim—
Nancy Cabot, *Chicago Tribune* 1933

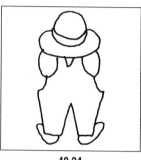

48.24
D Farmer Boy—
Frank's

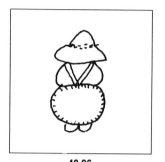

48.26
D Unnamed—
Sears, Roebuck and Co. 1934
(alternates with #55.82)

48.28
D Recollect—
Eveline Johnson in
Needlecraft Magazine 1938

48.32
D Overall Andy—
McKim, *Designs Worth Doing* #473

48.36
D Overall Andy—
McKim, *Designs Worth Doing* #473

48.4
D Romper Boy—
Rainbow

48.52
D Fisher Lad—
Wheeler/Brooks

48.54
D Fisher Boy—
Wheeler/Brooks #5025

48.6
D Happy Jack—
Nancy Cabot, *Chicago Tribune* 1936

48.7
D Farmer Boy—
Hagerman attributes to
duBarry ca. 1935

48.8
D Unnamed—
Hagerman pg. 31

49.12
D Cowgirl—
Aunt Ellen (Aunt Martha)

49.13
D Cowboy—
Aunt Ellen (Aunt Martha)

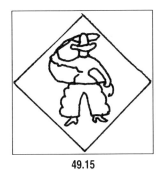

49.15
D Cowboy and Horse—
Wheeler/Brooks #770 (these were
sold as a series and individually;
there were more in the series than
are pictured here)

49.16
D Cowboy and Horse—
Wheeler/Brooks #770

49.17
D Cowboy—
Wheeler/Brooks #7025 and 7131

49.18
D Cowboy and Horse—
Wheeler/Brooks #7353

49.22
D Bronco Buster—
Needlecraft Magazine 1929

49.24
D Wild West Quilt—
Wheeler/Brooks #7566

49.32
T Unnamed—
from a quilt ca. 1900 from
Pennsylvania

49.34
D Squaw Quilt—
Hagerman #W-65

49.35
D Indian Princess—
Betty Royal in *Stitch 'n Sew* 8/1983

49.42
D Aunt Jemima—
from a quilt ca. 1935

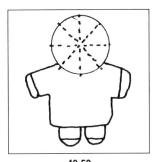

49.52
D Unnamed—
from a quilt ca. 1933

49.54
D Acrobats—
Nancy Cabot, *Chicago Tribune* 1937

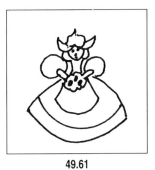

49.61
D Dutch Lass—
Nancy Cabot, *Chicago Tribune* 1938

49.62
D Dutch Girls—
Wheeler/Brooks #2054

49.63
D Dutch Boy—
Wheeler/Brooks #2054

49.64
D Toy Soldiers—
Wheeler/Brooks #7148

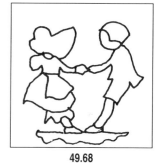

49.66
D Little Dutch Boy—
Nancy Cabot, *Chicago Tribune* 1933

49.68
D Dutch Boy and Girl—
Nancy Cabot, *Chicago Tribune* 1935

49.72
D Bo Peep—
McKim, *Designs Worth Doing* #265

49.73
D Boy Blue—
McKim, *Designs Worth Doing* #264

49.75
D Unnamed—
Sophie LaCroix

49.78
D Early to Bed—
Nancy Cabot, *Chicago Tribune* 1935

49.82
D Paper Doll—
Wheeler/Brooks

49.85
D Dotty, the Paper Doll Girl—
Woman's Home Companion 1931

49.86
D Dicky, the Paper Doll Boy—
Woman's Home Companion 1931

Miscellaneous Humans 50

50.1
T Unnamed—
from an album dated 1854

50.2
T Unnamed—
from an album dated 1844

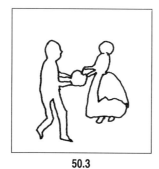

50.3
T Adam and Eve—
from a quilt ca. 1875

50.4
T The Creation of the Animals—
from a quilt by Harriett Powers ca.
1898 in the Smithsonian Institution

50.8
Hallowe'en Block—
Ladies Art Company #496

51.12
D Butterfly—
Nancy Cabot, *Chicago Tribune* 1933

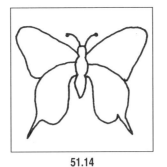

51.14
D Fancy Butterfly—
Grandmother Clark

51.16
D Plain Butterfly—
Grandmother Clark

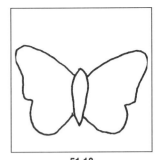

51.18
D Butterfly—
Boag

51.22
D Butterfly—
Wheeler/Brooks #C515

51.24
D Butterfly—
Nancy Cabot, *Chicago Tribune* 1936

51.26
D Butterfly—
Rainbow

51.28
D Butterflies—
Wheeler/Brooks #768

51.32
D Butterflies—
Wheeler/Brooks #768

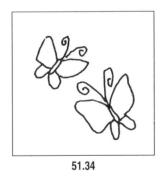

51.34
D Butterfly Applique—
Wheeler/Brooks #7462

51.35
D Gay Butterflies—
Wheeler/Brooks

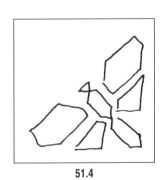

51.4
D Firefly—
Nancy Cabot, *Chicago Tribune* 1936

51.52
D Unnamed—
McCall's Needlework

51.54
D Butterfly and Flower—
Wheeler/Brooks 7246

51.62
D Butterfly Garden—
Rainbow #713

51.64
D Unnamed—
Rainbow #725

51.66
D Morning Glories—
Rainbow #731 and #847

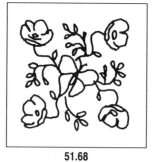

51.68
D Four Poppies and Butterflies—
Rainbow #808

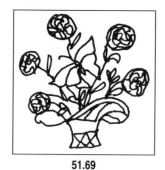

51.69
D Unnamed—
Rainbow #728

51.72
T Butterfly—
Rural New Yorker

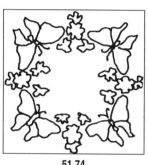

51.74
D Butterfly—
Ladies Art Company #6007

51.76
D Butterflies—
Ladies Art Company #414

51.78
T Unnamed—
from an album dated 1850

51.8
D Butterflies—
from a quilt ca. 1935 Woodard and
Greenstein/20th Century pg. 66

Birds 52-54

52.12
D Dove Applique—
Wheeler/Brooks

52.14
T Flying Bird—
Wilkinson

52.15
T Bluebird—
Nancy Cabot, *Chicago Tribune* 1944

52.16
D Unnamed—
Sears, Roebuck and Co. 1934

52.17
D Unnamed—
Rainbow #452

52.18
T Unnamed—
from an album dated 1847

52.19
D Bluebird Quilt—
Wheeler/Brooks

52.22
D Bird Quilt—
Wheeler/Brooks

52.24
D Curious Chicks—
Modern Priscilla 1926 (alternates
with a flower)

52.25
D Robin—
Nancy Cabot, *Chicago Tribune* 1934

52.26
D Red Bird—
Nancy Cabot, *Chicago Tribune* 1935

52.27
D Scarlet Song Bird—
Nancy Cabot, *Chicago Tribune*

52.28
T Pennsylvania Dutch Design—
Ickis, pg. 104

52.3
D Dickey Bird—
Wheeler/Brooks

52.42
D Yellow Warbler—
Rainbow #909F

52.44
D Cardinal and Morning Glory—
Rainbow #843

52.46
D Apple Blossoms—
Rainbow #858C

52.52
T Unnamed—
from an album dated 1854

52.54
T Unnamed—
from an album dated 1854

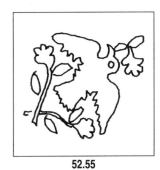

52.55
T Unnamed—
from a quilt in Bresenhan and
Puentes (Ark #59.4 is in center)

52.57
T Unnamed—
from an album dated 1849

52.59
T Unnamed—
from an album dated 1848

52.62
T Unnamed—
from an album dated 1861

52.64
T Unnamed—
from an album dated 1852

52.72

T Birds and Blossoms—
from a quilt in the
Quilt Engagement Calendar 1977,
plate 54

52.74

D Mr. Owl
Nancy Cabot, *Chicago Tribune*
Owl Block—
Nancy Cabot, *Chicago Tribune*
Wise Old Owl—
Nancy Cabot, *Chicago Tribune* 1938

52.76

D Owls in Applique—
Wheeler/Brooks #7508

52.82

T Two Doves—
unknown clipping
Bluebird—
Comfort

52.84

T Sweetheart Design—
Comfort

52.86

T Birds and Basket—
Comfort

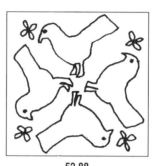

52.88

T Unnamed—
from an album dated 1847

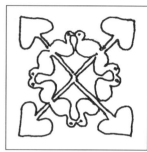

52.92

T Heart and Dove—
from a quilt ca. 1890
from Ulster, Ireland
Heart and Spade—
both names in use in Ulster

Poultry 53

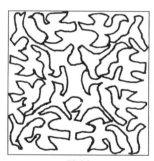

52.94

T Bluebird Design—
New York Press July 12, 1914

53.12

T Unnamed—
from an album dated 1865

53.14

D Little Chanticlear—
Nancy Cabot, *Chicago Tribune* 1938

53.16

D Unnamed—
Aunt Martha, *Prize-Winning Quilts*

53.18

D Chanticleer—
Mountain Mist #G

53.19

T Unnamed—
from an album dated 1854

53.22

D Chick in Boots—
Nancy Cabot, *Chicago Tribune* 1936

53.24

D Baby Chick—
Nancy Cabot, *Chicago Tribune* 1934

53.32
T Unnamed—
from an album dated 1865

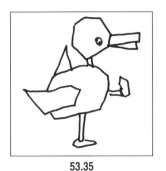

53.35
D Ducky Coverlet—
Farmer's Wife 6/1934

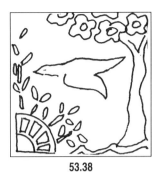

53.38
Wild Ducks—
Mountain Mist #45

53.42
D Just Ducky—
Wheeler/Brooks

53.44
D Ducky Doo—
Sears, Roebuck and Co. 1934
(alternates with #47.33)

53.46
D Unnamed—
Needlecraft Magazine 1929

53.52
D Unnamed—
Needlecraft Magazine 1932

53.53
D Unnamed—
Needlecraft Magazine 1932

53.6
D Flamingoes—
Nancy Cabot, *Chicago Tribune* 1936

53.72
D Mother Goose—
Nancy Cabot, *Chicago Tribune* 1934

53.74
D A Pair of Geese—
Nancy Cabot, *Chicago Tribune* 1934
A Pair of Ducklings—
Nancy Cabot, *Chicago Tribune* 1938

53.8
D Turkey and Pumpkin—
Wheeler/Brooks #5901N

Birds/Eagles 54

54.22
T Unnamed—
from an album dated 1855

54.23
T Unnamed—
from an album

54.3
T Unamed—
from a quilt dated 1917
(see #86.3)

54.4
T Unnamed—
from an album dated 1850

Birds/Eagles 54

54.5
T Unnamed—
from an album dated 1853

54.6
T Unnamed—
from an album dated 1852

54.72
T Eagle Applique—
Peto, *American Quilts*, pg. 42

54.8
T Unnamed—
from an album dated 1849

Dogs 55

55.13
D Unnamed—
Needlecraft Magazine 1929

55.15
D Scottie—
Needlecraft Magazine 1935

55.22
D Scottie—
Nancy Cabot, *Chicago Tribune* 1934

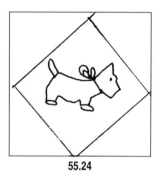

55.24
D Scottie Dog—
Wheeler/Brooks #1517

55.26
D Scotch Terriers—
Wheeler/Brooks #7145

55.28
D Humoristic Cat and Dog—
Vogue #2054

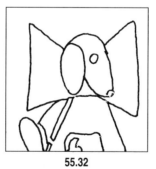

55.32
D Blue Ribbon Setter—
Nancy Cabot, *Chicago Tribune* 1936

55.35
D Frisky Dog—
Wheeler/Brooks

55.42
D Scottie—
Wheeler/Brooks
Puppy Applique—
Wheeler/Brooks #520

55.43
D Wirehaired Pup—
Nancy Cabot, *Chicago Tribune* 1935

55.51
D Puppy Blocks—
Wheeler/Brooks #7438

55.52
D Unnamed—
Sears, Roebuck and Co. 1934
(alternates with #48.26)

55.53
D Little Bowser—
Nancy Cabot, *Chicago Tribune* 1935

55.54
D Doggie Applique—
Wheeler/Brooks #1846

55.55
D Dog Applique—
Wheeler/Brooks #2216

55.56
D Puppies—
Wheeler/Brooks #7260

Cats, Rabbits, Fish, etc. 56

56.11
D Kitten—
Nancy Cabot, *Chicago Tribune* 1934

56.12
D Kitten Applique—
Wheeler/Brooks #5963

56.13
D Calico Cat—
Wheeler/Brooks #1583

56.14
D Kitten Block—
Nancy Cabot, *Chicago Tribune* 1938

56.15
D Kitten—
Wheeler/Brooks #7260

56.16
D Nursery Patch—
Wheeler/Brooks

56.17
D Kitten Applique—
Wheeler/Brooks #1988

56.18
D Breakfast—
Nancy Cabot, *Chicago Tribune* 1938

56.2
D Teddy Bear—
Wheeler/Brooks #2916

56.23
D Teddy Bear—
Wheeler/Brooks

56.26
D Teddy Bear—
Nancy Cabot, *Chicago Tribune* 1934

56.32
D Appliqued Bunny—
Wilkinson

56.33
D Bunny Applique—
Wheeler/Brooks #1876

56.34
D Peter Rabbit in his Garden—
Nancy Cabot, *Chicago Tribune*

56.35
D Jack Rabbit—
Nancy Cabot, *Chicago Tribune* 1938

56.37
D Bunnies—
Webster design 1914
(alternates with basket)

56.42
D Elephant—
Needlecraft Magazine 1929

56.43
D Little Jumbo—
Nancy Cabot, *Chicago Tribune* 1935

56.44
D Old Jumbo—
Nancy Cabot, *Chicago Tribune* 1938

56.45
D Elephant Applique—
Wheeler/Brooks #1621

56.46
D Dancing Jumbo—
Nancy Cabot, *Chicago Tribune* 1936

56.47
D Elephant—
Nancy Cabot, *Chicago Tribune* 1935

56.48
D Lucky Elephant—
Vogue #2053

56.52
D Buddy Squirrel—
Nancy Cabot, *Chicago Tribune* 1934
Papa Squirrel—
Nancy Cabot, *Chicago Tribune* 1938

56.54
D Little Omar—
Nancy Cabot, *Chicago Tribune* 1938

56.55
D Lamb—
Nancy Cabot, *Chicago Tribune* 1934

56.58
D Hobby Horse—
Nancy Cabot, *Chicago Tribune* 1938

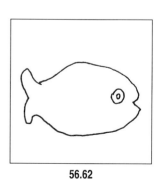

56.62
D Jonah's Fish—
Nancy Cabot, *Chicago Tribune* 1936

Cats, Rabbits, Fish, etc. 56

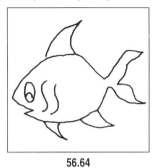

56.64
D Baby Shark—
Nancy Cabot, *Chicago Tribune* 1936

56.66
D Bias Tape Motif—
Wheeler/Brooks #7400

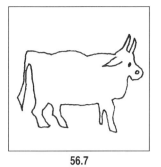

56.7
T Unnamed—
from an album dated 1857

56.8
T Unnamed—
from an album dated 1865

Trees 57

56.9
T Unnamed—
from an album dated 1854

57.1
T Forest Bride's Quilt—
from a quilt dated 1861
in the Art Institute of Chicago

57.3
T Unnamed—
from a quilt in the
Quilt Engagement Calendar 1978,
plate 39

57.4
D Trees and Garlands—
alternates with wreath in Paragon kit

57.5
T Tree of Life—
from a quilt ca. 1850 in
Quilts of Tennessee, pg. 50

57.6
T Cherry Trees—
Paragon kit, a copy of a quilt ca.
1850 in the Art Institute of Chicago

57.7
D Evergreen Tree—
Nancy Cabot, *Chicago Tribune* 1936

57.8
D Palm Tree—
Nancy Cabot, *Chicago Tribune*

Houses and Buildings 58

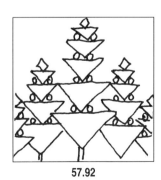

57.92
D Sheltering Pines—
Nancy Cabot, *Chicago Tribune* 1936

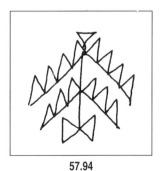

57.94
D Monday's Trees—
Nancy Cabot, *Chicago Tribune* 1936

58.12
D Unnamed—
Needlecraft Magazine

58.13
D Unnamed—
Needlecraft Magazine 1923

58.14
D Unnamed—
Needlecraft Magazine 1923

58.15
D Sunnyside—
Modern Priscilla August, 1928

58.16
D Enchanted Cottage—
Wheeler/Brooks #726

58.17
D Homestead—
Wheeler/Brooks #1576
Little Village—
Wheeler/Brooks #1576

58.18
D The Cottage Behind the Hill—
Aunt Martha, *Prize-Winning Quilts*

58.2
D Unnamed—
Sears, Roebuck and Co., 1934

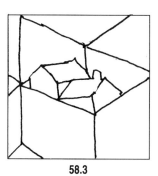

58.3
D House and Hill—
Nancy Cabot, *Chicago Tribune*

58.4
T Unnamed—
from an album dated 1852

Boats 59

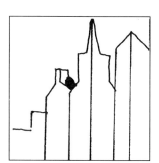

58.5
D Skyscraper—
Successful Farming

59.13
D Red Sails—
Nancy Cabot, *Chicago Tribune*

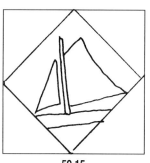

59.15
D Sailboat—
Wheeler/Brooks #1549

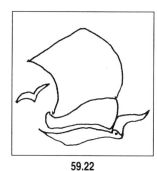

59.22
D The Sea Gull—
Needlecraft Magazine 1933

59.24
D Dream Ship—
Nancy Cabot, *Chicago Tribune* 1935

59.25
D Treasure Ship—
Needlecraft Magazine 1935

59.3
T Unnamed—
from an album dated 1849

59.4
T Unnamed—
from a quilt in Bresenhan and
Puentes, combined with dove
#52.55

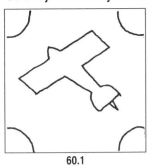

60.1
D The Airplane—
Nancy Cabot, *Chicago Tribune*

60.22
D Bedtime—
Nancy Cabot, *Chicago Tribune* 1936

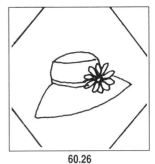

60.24
T Unnamed—
from an album dated 1846

60.26
D Unnamed—
Wheeler/Brooks

60.32
T Unnamed—
from an album dated 1853

60.35
T Unnamed—
from an album dated 1865

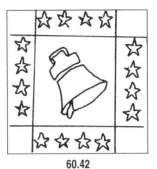

60.42
D Centennial—
Nancy Cabot, *Chicago Tribune*

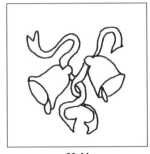

60.44
D Bells of St. Mary's—
Nancy Cabot, *Chicago Tribune* 1939

60.51
T Unnamed—
from an album dated 1865

60.53
T The Valentine Quilt—
Kansas City Star 1955

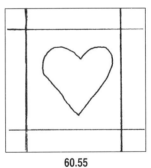

60.55
D The Bleeding Heart—
Kansas City Star 1950

60.56
T Gift of Love—
Finley, pg. 190

60.59
D Valentines—
Nancy Cabot, *Chicago Tribune* 1936

60.62
T Unnamed—
from an album dated 1850

60.64
T Unnamed—
from an album dated 1852

60.66
T Unnamed—
from an album dated 1865

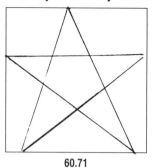

60.71
D Eastern Star—
Nancy Cabot, *Chicago Tribune* 1935

60.72
T Unnamed—
from an album dated 1852

60.74
T Unnamed—
from an album dated 1860

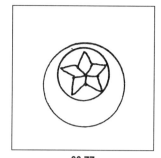

60.77
T Star and Crescent—
Wilkinson

60.78
T Crescent Moon—
Hearth and Home

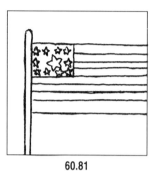

60.81
T Unnamed—
from an album dated 1865

60.82
T Unnamed—
from an album dated 1861

60.83
T Unnamed—
from an album dated 1859

60.84
T Unnamed—
from an album dated 1867

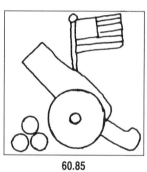

60.85
D Fourth of July—
Nancy Cabot, *Chicago Tribune* 1936

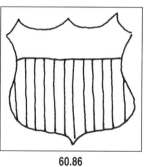

60.86
T Shield—
Ladies Art Company #420

60.87
T Unnamed—
from an album dated 1859

60.88
T Unnamed—
from an album dated 1861

60.92
T Unnamed—
from an album ca. 1860
(Odd Fellow's Chain)

60.94
T Unnamed—
from an album ca. 1850
(Odd Fellow's Chain)

60.96
T Unnamed—
from a quilt ca. 1858
(Masonic symbol)

71.3 D Falling Leaves—Nancy Page 1936 (18 leaves) See #43

72.3 D Coverlet in Floral Design—*Needlecraft Magazine* 1934 (4 flowers)

72.5 D Laurel Wreath—Nancy Page 1934 (30 blocks)

71.5 D Leaf Quilt—Nancy Page 1931 (4 leaves) See #5.1

72.1 D Four Flowers Set— Wheeler/Brooks (3 flowers pictured)

72.2 D Flower Garden—Home Art (10 flowers) Aunt Susan's Flower Garden—Home Art

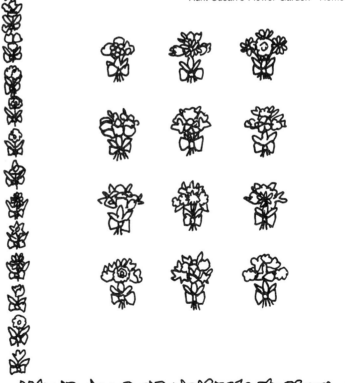

72.4 D French Bouquet—Nancy Page 1933 (12 bouquets, 15 border blocks)

72.6 D Hearts and Flowers—
Nancy Page 1938 (4 blocks)

72.7 D Modernistic Flower—*Portland Oregonian* (28 blocks)

72.82 D Unnamed—Rainbow stamped block
set #500v (12 blocks) See #34.75

Containers, Fruit and Wreaths 73

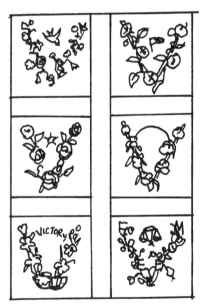

72.84 D The Victory Quilt—Rainbow
stamped block ca. 1943 (6 blocks)

72.9 D Flower Garden—
McKim 1929–1930 (25 blocks)

73.12 D Garden Bouquet—Nancy Page 1931
(20 blocks) See 42.35

73.13 D Quilt of Birds—
Needlecraft Magazine 1937

73.2 D Flower Basket—Aunt Martha (12 blocks)

73.3 D Flower Bowl—
Wheeler/Brooks #208 (6 blocks)

73.4 D Memory Bouquet—Eveline Foland 1930
(20 blocks in *Kansas City Star*, 25 in *Detroit News*)

73.5 D Flower Pot Combination—
Herschnners (5 blocks) See 39.7

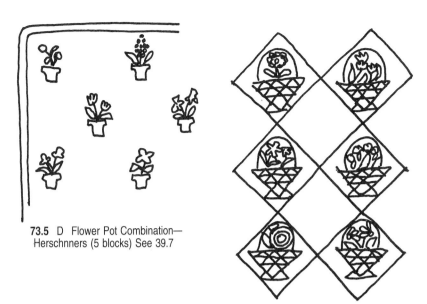

73.6 D Fruit Basket Quilt—McKim 1929–1930 (32 baskets)

73.7 D Grandmother's Garden—Nancy Page 1928 (20 baskets)

73.82 D Horn of Plenty—Eveline Foland in *Kansas City Star* 1932 (18 fruits)

73.84 D Garden Fruits—Nancy Page 1935 (10 fruits)

73.9 T Wreath—Nancy Page 1931 (4)

74.12 D Sunbonnet Sue—McKim/Designs Worth Doing (3 figures)

74.13 D Children's Nursery Blocks—Rainbow stamped block set #715 (6 figures)

74.15 D Sunbonnet Babies—Herschnners #3581 (12 figures)

74.17 D Mother Goose Quilt—Nancy Page 1938 (9 figures)

74.18 D Sunbonnet Girl—Grandma Dexter (6 figures)

74.19 D Overall Boy—Grandma Dexter (6 figures)

74.21 D Colonial Lady—Grandma Dexter (6 figures) See 47.9

150

74.23 D Sunbonnet Girls—Wheeler/Brooks #7027

74.3 D 1-2 Buckle My Shoe—Nancy Page 1937 (10 blocks)

74.25 D Colonial Belle—*Capper's Weekly* (12 blocks)

74.4 D Mother Goose—McKim (12 blocks)

74.5 D Bible Quilt—*Ladies Home Journal* #1503 (12 blocks)

74.6 D Little Brown KoKo—*Capper's Weekly*

Objects and Animals 75

75.13 D Story Book Quilt—Marion Cheever Whiteside in *McCalls* (12 blocks)

75.15 D Three Little Kittens—Ladies Art Company #6068 (8 blocks)

75.17 D Pussy Cat—Herschnner

75.23 D Crib Cover—Famous Features #2732

75.24 D Crib of Sleepy Time Pets—*Capper's Weekly* 1935 (8 blocks)

75.26 D Animal Crib Quilt—Wheeler/Brooks #7009

75.3 D Three Little Pigs—McKim 1934 (13 blocks)

75.4 D Teddy Bear—Herschnner #3613

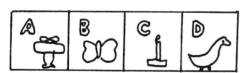

75.51 D ABC Quilt—Boag kit 1933 (24 blocks)

75.52 D Toy Shop Window—McKim 1933–1934 (12 blocks)

75.54 D Alphabet Quilt—Nancy Page 1929 (24 blocks)

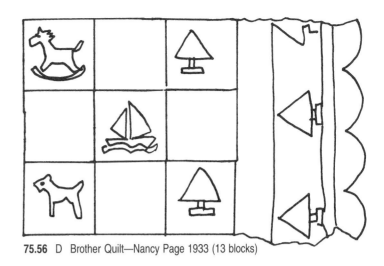

75.56 D Brother Quilt—Nancy Page 1933 (13 blocks)

75.57 D Sister Quilt—Nancy Page 1933 (13 blocks)

75.59 D Christmas Toy Quilt—Aileen Bullard in *Kansas City Star* 1932 (13 blocks)

75.62 D Quilt of Birds—Nancy Page 1937 (12 birds)

75.64 D Birds—*Quilter's Newsletter Magazine* ca 1973 (4 birds)

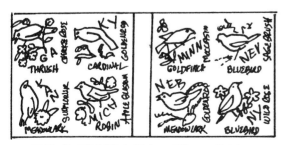

75.66 D Official State Birds and Flower—Rainbow

75.68 D Audubon or Bird Life Quilt—McKim 1928–1929

153

75.72 D Calendar Quilt—Nancy Page 1935 (12 months)

75.74 D Old Almanac—Nancy Page 1932 (12 signs)

75.82 D Snowflake Quilt—Nancy Page 1932 (12 blocks)

75.9 D Sunflower Bedspread—attributed to John Then in *McCalls*

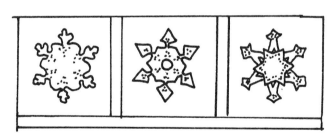

75.84 D Pretty Snowflake—Rainbow stamped block set #733 (6 blocks) See also snowflakes numbered 36.6

80.12 D Floral Basket—*Needlecraft Magazine*

80.13 D Dogwood Basket—Ladies Art Company

80.11 D Flower Garden—Lockport

80.15 D Spring Basket—*Needlecraft Magazine*
Spring Bouquet—Herschnner

80.14 D Old Fashioned May Basket—*Needlecraft Magazine*

80.16 D Lady Sheridan—Home Needlecraft Creations

80.17 D The Applique Basket—Anne Orr

80.22 T Indiana Wreath—*McCalls* ca. 1935

80.23 T Indiana Wreath—name inscribed on quilt dated 1858 in Webster

80.24 D June Basket—Home Needlecraft Creations kit #7168

80.31 D Basket of Roses—Mrs. Danner Books 1 & 2

80.33 D Unnamed—from a quilt ca. 1935 in *Quilt Engagement Calendar* 1992, plate 19

80.34 D Poppy Basket—Boag kit

80.41 D Cape Cod Basket—Source not found

80.42 D Poppy Basket—Ladies Art Company

80.43 D French Basket—St. Louis Fancy Work

80.44 D Pink Dogwood in Baskets—Webster

80.46 D Baskets and Wild Roses—St. Louis Fancy Work

80.47 D Garland and Basket—
Ann Orr in *Good Housekeeping*

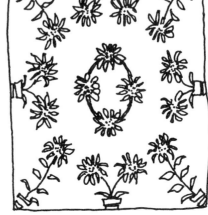

80.48 D Four Baskets—*Needlecraft Magazine*

80.49 D Poinsettia—Mountain Mist

81.1 D Crib Quilt Design—*Modern Priscilla* 1924

81. 2 D American Beauty—*McCalls*

81.23 D Poppy—*Capper's Weekly*

81.4 D Sunflower—*Capper's Weekly*

81.5 D Daisy Chain—Mary McElwain 1936

81.63 D First Lady—
Needlecraft Supply

81.65 D American Beauty Bouquet—Gold Art Needlework,
also Homeneedlecraft Creations #7452

81.71 D Orchid Wreath—Rose Kretsinger in Hall and Kretsinger

81.73 D Morning Glory—Webster

81.75 D Morning Glory—Webster

81.76 T Tulip Wreath—*Ladies Home Journal 1912* Conventional Flower Design—*Modern Priscilla* 1925

81.77 D Morning Glories—Nancy Cabot, *Chicago Tribune* 1935

81.81 D Unnamed—*Woman's World*

81.92 T Wreath of Roses—Hall and Kretsinger pg. 187

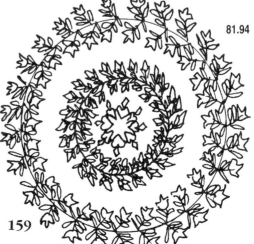

81.94 T Wreath and Star—Ickis pg. 24

82.13 D Climbing Rose—Herschnner kit

82.15 D Old Fashioned Bouquet—Ladies Art Company #6080

82.17 D White House Quilt—*Needlecraft Magazine* 1937
Cape Cod Quilt—*McCalls* Lady Delano—Homeneedlecraft Creations

82.21 D Marie Antoinette—Herschnner

82.22 D Spring Bouquet—Needlecraft kit #3575

82.23 D Pansy Bed—Needlecraft kit #3576

82.24 D Rose Bouquet—Herschnner

82.25 D Formal Garden—Needlecraft kit #3555

82.26 D Old Fashioned Spray—Anne Orr in *Good Housekeeping*

82.27 D Rose and Bowknot—Anne Orr in *Good Housekeeping*

82.28 D Old Sampler Quilt—Anne Orr in *Good Housekeeping* 1937

82.29 D Unnamed—from a quilt ca. 1940 (probably a kit)

82.31 D Pansy—McKim/*101 Quilt Patterns*, pg. 97

82.32 D Pansies—*Capper's Weekly*

82.33 D Pansy—Progress kit #1365

82.41 D Poppy Wreath—Mountain Mist

82.42 D Poppy—Anne Orr in *Good Housekeeping*

82.44 D Painted Poppies—Mountain Mist

82.46 D Poppy Design—Webster

82.48 D Poppy—Boag kit

82.51 D Climbing Rose—Lockport Batting

162

82.54 D Unnamed—
Nancy Cabot, *Chicago Tribune* 1935

82.62 D Unnamed—Bucilla kit

82.63 D Morning Glory—*McCalls* 1928

82.65 D Morning Glory—Mrs. Danner Books 1 & 2

82.66 D Morning Glory Vine Scroll—Needlecraft kit

82.711 D The Sunflower—Mountain Mist

82.712 D The Sunflower Quilt—Webster

82.72 D Tiger Lily—from a quilt ca. 1940
in Clark/Ohio, pg. 104

82.73 D Gladiola—from a quilt 1946
in Nebraska, pg. 46

82.74 D Carnation—from a quilt ca. 1940 in *Quilt Engagement Calendar* 1992, plate 57 (probably a Progress kit)

82.75 D The Iris—Anne Orr

82.76 D Iris Applique—Herschnner kit

82.77 D Spring—Boag kit

82.78 D April Showers—Mountain Mist #82

82.79 D The Garden—from a quilt 1857 in Finley, plate 57

82.81 D Provincial—Paragon kit

82.82 D Cluster of Roses—Webster

82.83 D Rose of Sharon—Mountain Mist

82.84 D Magnolia Blooms—Mountain Mist

82.85 D Columbine Quilt—*Needlecraft Magazine*
Columbine Special—*Rainbow #328*

82.86 D A Beautiful Patchwork Spread—
Home Needlework Magazine

82.87 D The Wild Rose—Boag kit

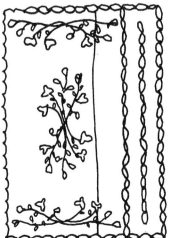

82.88 D Plymouth Garden—*McCalls*

82.89 D Unnamed—Wheeler/Brooks #565

82.91 D The Dolly Varden—Mrs. Danner Books 1 & 2

82.921 D Unknown—Anne Orr #A6601

82.923 D Roosevelt Rose—Finley in *Good Housekeeping*

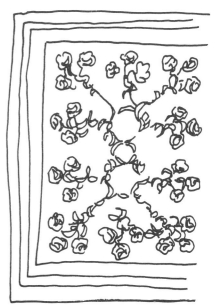

82.93 D American Beauty Climbing Rose—Source not found

82.94 D Wild Rose—Webster

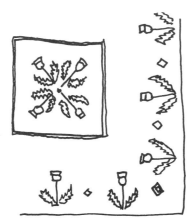

82.95 D Patches for a Man's Room—*Modern Priscilla* 1925

82.96 D Pansies—Nancy Cabot, *Chicago Tribune* 1935. See 86.15

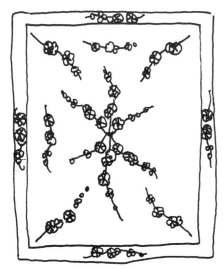

82.973 D Cherry Blossoms—Mountain Mist #104

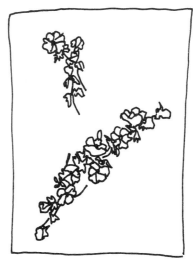

82.975 D Anemone—Mountain Mist #126

82.98 D The Initial Quilt—Anne Orr

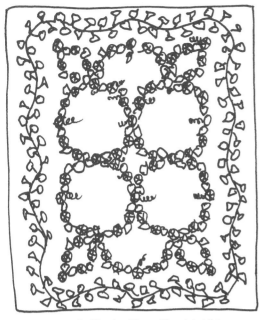

82.997 D Dogwood—Mountain Mist

82.992 D Morning Glory—Mountain Mist

82.994 D White Dogwood—Webster in *Ladies Home Journal* 1912 Dogwood Quilt—Webster

Medallions/Fruit 83

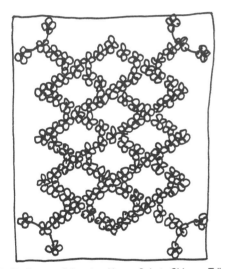

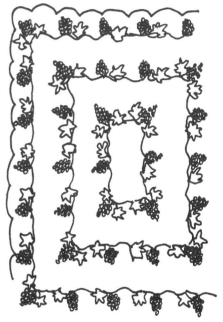

82.998 D Dogwood Beauty—Nancy Cabot, *Chicago Tribune*

83.1 D Orange Blossoms—Mountain Mist

83.22 D Wedgewood—Mrs. Danner

83.23 D Unnamed—from a quilt ca. 1940 in *Quilt Engagement Calendar* 1991, plate 40

84.1 T Unnamed—from a quilt ca. 1890 in Woodard and Greenstein/Crib Quilts, fig. 87

84.2 T Oak Leaves with Cherries—Kimball

84.4 T Unnamed—from a quilt dated 1818 in Spencer Museum

84.6 D Bachelor's Quilt—St. Louis Fancy Work #1216

85.13 D Bambino Spread—*Needlecraft Magazine* 1923

85.11 D Little Man in the Moon—Ladies Art Company

85.12 D Crib Blanket—*Needlecraft Magazine* 1926

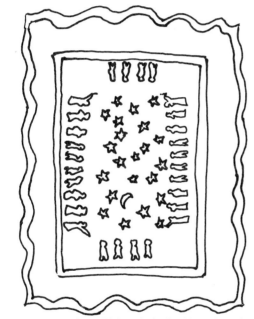

85.15 D Bedtime Quilt—Webster in *Ladies Home Journal* 1912

85.17 D Kiddies' Ride—Needlecraft kit

85.18 D Rock-a-Bye Baby—Colonial Art Needlework kit

85.21 D Little Miss Tiptoe—*Needlecraft Magazine*

85.22 D Mistress Betty—*Modern Priscilla* 1922

85.26 D Dutch Girl—Anne Orr in *Good Housekeeping*   **85.27** D Dutch Boy—Anne Orr in *Good Housekeeping*

85.31 D Keepsake Quilt—Webster in *Ladies Home Journal* 1912   **85.33** D Mother Goose—Boag kit   **85.35** D Small Fry—Mountain Mist

85.37 D Sun Bonnet Babe—Boag kit

85.42 D Old Woman in the Shoe—
Needlecraft Magazine

85.44 D Little Red Riding Hood—*Needlecraft Magazine*

85.49 D Cinderella—Needlecraft kit

85.5 D Hallo Een Quilt—Nancy Cabot,
Chicago Tribune 1935

86.13 D Butterflies—Mountain Mist

86.15 D Golden Butterflies and Pansies—Webster. See 82.96

86.21 D Bicentennial Quilt—Mrs. Danner

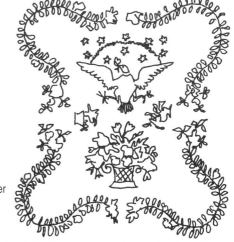

86.23 T Unnamed—one of several similar quilts made
in Maryland ca. 1830. Border is reverse applique

86.24 T American Glory—Paragon kit (drawn after quilt ca. 1850)

86.25 T Spread Eagle—*Omaha World Herald* 1912

86.3 T Unnamed—numerous examples ca. 1880, common in Pennsylvania

86.41 D Unnamed—*McCalls* #2701D

86.42 D Unknown—from a clipping 1916

86.43 D Three Little Kittens—Source not found

86.44 D Unknown—Source not found

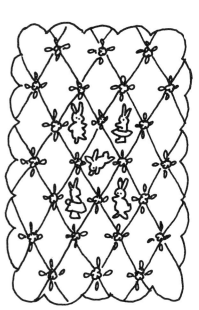

86.52 D Bunnies—Needlecraft kit

86.53 D Bunnies—Mountain Mist

86.54 D Unnamed—Anne Orr

86.55 D Bedtime Bunnies—*Modern Priscilla* kit 1927

86.6 D Unknown—
kit source not found

86.71 D Noah's Ark—source not found

86.72 D Noah's Ark—Designs Worth Doing

86.74 D Unnamed—*McCalls*

86.8 D The Elephant's Child—
E. Buckner Kirk in *Woman's Home Companion* 1934

Medallions/Patriotic 87

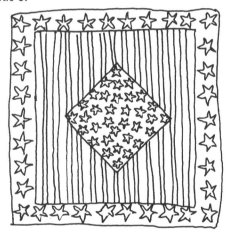

87.1 T A Patriotic Quilt—*Peterson's Magazine* May/June 1861

87.2 T Flag—from a quilt 1932 in Woodard and
Greenstein/*20th Century*, pg. 99

87.33 T Flags and Shields—from a quilt 1921, Kansas Quilt Project

87.35 T Unnamed—from a quilt 1898 in Bishop and Houck

88.12 D Autumn Leaf—Anne Orr 1932

88.14 D Autumn Leaves—Nancy Cabot, *Chicago Tribune* and Sears

88.15 D Tree of Life—McKim

88.17 D Autumn Leaves—Needlecraft Supply Co. kit 1935

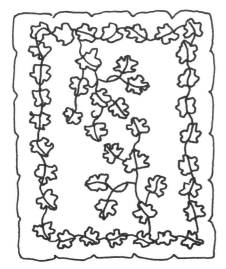

88.3 D Family Tree—
Wheeler/Brooks #799 ca. 1975

88.4 D North Across the Border—*McCalls*

88.2 D Trailing Leaf—Home Needlecraft kit

88.5 D Christmas Tree Quilt—*Needlecraft Magazine* 1924

88.6 D American Heritage—Bucilla kit #1894

88.72 D Rose Tree—Mountain Mist. See 37.246

88.74 D Blossom Time—
Homeneedlecraft Creations #7066

88.8 D Tree of Life—Progress kit #1369

Medallions/Miscellaneous Pictorial

89.2 D Early American—Paragon kit

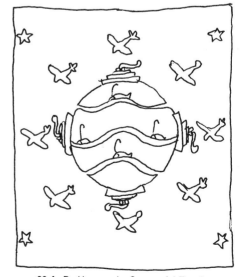

89.4 D Unnamed—*Successful Farming*

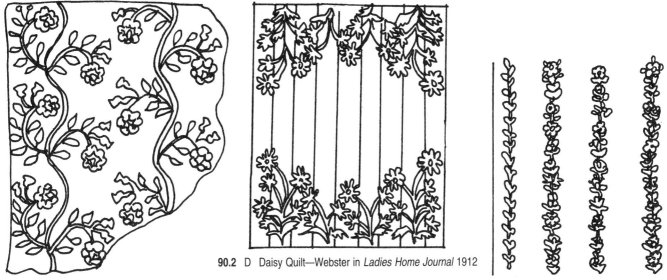

90.2 D Daisy Quilt—Webster in *Ladies Home Journal* 1912

90.1 T Rose of Sharon—from a quilt in Havig/Missouri, pg. 71

90.31 D Magic Vine—Nancy Page 1930

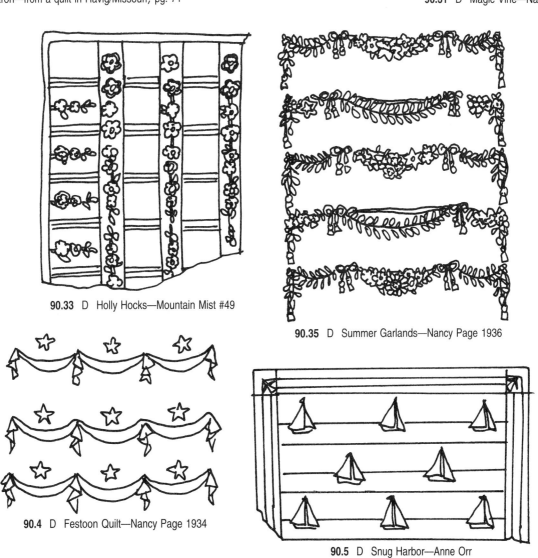

90.33 D Holly Hocks—Mountain Mist #49

90.35 D Summer Garlands—Nancy Page 1936

90.4 D Festoon Quilt—Nancy Page 1934

90.5 D Snug Harbor—Anne Orr

91.1 T Rocky Mountain—*Ladies Home Journal* 7/1909
The Great Divide—*Ladies Home Journal* 7/1909
See as a pieced design #1083 and as applique #25.9

91.2 T Unnamed—from a quilt dated 1874

91.3 T Vining New York Beauty—Texas Heritage Quilt Society

References for Indexed Patterns

Album. Refers to an album or friendship quilt, usually with an inscribed date.

Arkansas Quilters Guild. Arkansas Quilts, (Paducah, KY: American Quilters Society).

Aunt Martha Studios. Booklets, kits and related items are still offered by Kansas City's Colonial Patterns, Inc. The company began in the early 1930s when they were advertised in a syndicated column under various names including Aunt Ellen, Aunt Matilda, Betsy Ross, Royal Neighbor and Colonial Quilt. Aunt Martha was the most common name used. In 1949 Colonial Patterns and Workbasket split. Current Address: Colonial Patterns, Inc., 340 W 5th St., Kansas City, MO 64105-1235.

Aunt Martha Booklets:

>*A New & Easy Way to Make a Quilt* (ca. 1931)
>*Favorites Old and New* (#5511, ca. 1932)
>*Prize-Winning Designs* (#300, ca. 1933)
>*Quilt Fair Comes to You* (#5514, ca. 1933)
>*Star Designs* (#9450, ca. 1942)
>*Quilt Designs, Old Favorites and New* (#3175)
>*Aunt Martha's Favorite Quilts* (#3230)
>*Quilts Modern and Colonial* (#3333)
>*Easy Quilts* (#3500)
>*Quilt Lover's Delight* (#3540)
>*Quilts* (#3614)
>*Bold & Beautiful Quilts* (#3778)
>*Patchwork Simplicity* (#3779) (also called *Patchwork, Plain & Simple*)
>*Quilts: Heirlooms of Tomorrow* (#3788)

Bishop, Robert. The Knopf Collector's Guides to American Antiques, *Quilts, Coverlets, Rugs & Samplers.* (New York: Alfred A. Knopf, 1982).

Bishop, Robert, and Patricia Coblentz. *New Discoveries in American Quilts* (New York: E.P. Dutton, 1975).

Bishop, Robert, and Carter Houck. *All Flags Flying* (New York: E.P. Dutton, 1986).

Boag. A kit company circa 1935 from Elgin, Illinois.

Bresenhan, Karoline Patterson and Nancy O'Bryant Puentes, *Lone Star: A Legacy of Texas Quilts,* 1836-1936 (Austin, TX: University of Texas Press, 1986).

Brooks, Alice, See Wheeler, Laura.

Bucilla. A kit company that may still be in business. Sold kits through several magazines and Herrschner's catalog.

Bureau Farmer*.* Periodical from the American Farm Bureau Federation from 1925-35.

Cabot, Nancy. Syndicated column written by Loretta Leitner Rising for the *Chicago Tribune* beginning January, 1933. There were hundreds of Cabot patterns that were sold mail-order and grouped in booklets through the 1930s and 1940s. The same patterns were also sold by the Spinning Wheel syndicate and the *Progressive Farmer.* Patterns were reprinted in the 1960s and '70s by several small publishers but are currently out-of-print again, as far as I know.

Capper's Weekly*.* A periodical from Topeka's Capper Publications, which has published the weekly newspaper since 1879. From 1927 through 1935 they offered a unique column authored by staff member Louise Fowler Roote, who wrote under the name Kate Marchbanks, the fictitious editor of the women's page, titled "In the Heart of the Home." Since 1935 they have offered various syndicated columns, particularly "Famous Features" (see entry), which incorporated some of Roote's designs. Other Capper publications that printed quilt patterns were the *Kansas Farmer, Capper's Farmer, Capper's Farm Press, The Mail & Breeze,* and *The Household Magazine.*

Chicago Art Institute. Davison, Mildred, *American Quilts 1819-1948 from the Museum Collection,* (Chicago: The Art Institute of Chicago, 1959).

Clark, Grandmother. A series of booklets from the W.L.M. Clark Inc. of St. Louis that also published booklets on crocheting, tatting etc. and sold quilt kits. One other name occasionally used was Winifred Clark. The company began publishing quilt patterns in the early 1930s, and continued selling stamped needlework items into the 1950s.

Grandmother Clark booklets:

>*Grandmother Clark's Patchwork Quilts* (#19, 1932)
>*Grandmother Clark's Patchwork Quilt Designs* (#20, 1931)
>*Grandmother Clark's Old Fashioned Quilt Designs* (#21, 1931)

Grandmother Clark's Quilting Designs
(#22)
*Grandmother Clark's Authentic Early
American Patchwork Quilts* (#23)

Clark, Ricky, George W. Knepper and Ellice Ronsheim. *Quilts in Community, Ohio's Traditions* (Nashville: Rutledge Hill, 1991).

Clarke, Mary Washington. *Kentucky Quilts and Their Makers* (Lexington: University Press of Kentucky, 1976).

Coats and Clark. Thread manufacturer that published at least two pattern books:

Quilts (#1145,S-22, 1945)
Heirloom Quilts (#160)

Comfort. Periodical published from 1888 to 1942 in Augusta, Maine by Gannet and Morse. *Comfort* published many patterns in the magazine, sold them mail-order and published at least one booklet, *Comfort's Applique and Patchwork: Revival of Old Time Patchwork* (1921 or 1922), edited by Mrs. Wheeler Wilkinson. It contained many of the *Comfort* designs in this index.

Country Gentleman. A periodical founded as *Gennessee Farmer* in the early 19th century. Became *Country Gentleman* in 1853; changed to *Better Farming* in 1955 and merged with *Farm Journal* that year. In the 1930s sold mail-order patterns and published articles by Velma Mackey Paul and Florence LaGanke Harris, among others.

Country Home. Periodical that published patterns in the 1930s.

Country Life. Periodical that published patterns near the turn of the century.

Crews, Patricia Cox and Ronald C. Naugle (eds.). *Nebraska Quilts* (Lincoln: University of Nebraska Press, 1991).

Danner, Scioto Imhoff. She started a mail-order pattern source known as Mrs. Danner's Quilts in 1934. Helen Ericson bought the company in 1970. Danner pubished four pamphlets and Ericson has added four more. All currently available from Mrs. Danner's Quilts, Box 650, Emporia, KS 66801.

Davis, Carolyn O'Bagy. *Pioneer Quiltmaker: The Story of Dorinda Moody Slade* (Tucson: Sanpete Publications, 1990).

Denver Art Museum has published several catalogs: Among them: DeGraw, Imelda, *Quilts and Coverlets, 1974.* The collection includes several quilts donated by Charlotte Whitehill, copied from traditional patterns in the mid-twentieth century.

Dexter, Grandma. Series of booklets published in the early 1930s from the Virginia Snow Studios, a part of the Dexter Yarn and Thread Company and the Collingbourne Mills in Elgin, Illinois. Some syndicated column advertisements apeared (the one I have is from the *Missouri Farm Bureau News*).

The Grandma Dexter booklets:

Grandma Dexter's Applique and Patchwork Quilt Designs (#36)
Grandma Dexter's Applique and Patchwork Designs (#36A)
Grandma Dexter's New Applique and Patchwork Designs (#36B)

Famous Features. A syndicated, mail-order source that still sells pattern booklets from a New York address. Some pattern collectors call them the Q Books since each number is preceded by a Q. They appear to have begun in the 1940s, probably an outgrowth of *Capper's Weekly* patterns (see entry). Mabel Obenchain is the author most commonly mentioned.

Famous Features booklets:

Flower Quilts (#Q 101)
Grandmother's Patchwork Quilts (#Q 103)
All Year Quilts (#Q 103)
Young Folks Quilts (#Q 104)
Covered Wagon Quilts (#Q 105)
Bible Favorites (#Q 106)
A B C Quilts (#Q107)
Centennial Quilts (#Q 108)
Early American Quilts (#Q 109)
Star Quilts (#Q 110)
Round the World Quilts (#Q 111)
One Piece Quilts (#Q 112)
Blue Ribbon Quilts (#Q 116)
Quilts on Parade (also *Parade of Quilts*)
(#Q 117)
Grandmother's Flower Quilts (#Q 118)
Bicentennial Quilts (#Q 121)
White House Quilts (#Q 124)

Rose Quilts (#Q 125)
All Time Favorites (#Q 126)
Keepsake Quilts (#Q 130)

Farm and Fireside. Periodical published by Crowell in Springfield, Ohio. Patterns began in 1884 and are among the earliest periodical series.

Farm and Home. Periodical that printed patterns after the mid 1880s.

Farm Journal. Periodical established in March, 1877 and still publishing. They have absorbed at least three other pattern sources (*Country Gentleman, The Farmer's Wife* and *Household Journal*). In the 20th century they have offered mail-order patterns and booklets. Some of the patterns are reproduced in Rachel Martens' *Modern Patchwork* (Philadelphia: Countryside Press, 1970).

Farmer's Wife, The. Periodical published in St. Paul, MN from the 19th century through 1939 when it merged with *Farm Journal*.

Booklets include:

Lorene Dunnigan, *Quilts* (ca. 1930)
Orrine Johnson and Eleanor C. Lewis, *The Farmer's Wife Book of Quilts* (1931)
Orrine Johnson and Eleanor C Lewis, *Farmer's Wife Quilts: A New Book of Patterns* (1932).
Farmer's Wife Book of Quilts IV (1937).

Family, The. A magazine that has not yet been documented. I have one 1913 clipping with several applique patterns.

Finley, Ruth. *Old Patchwork Quilts and the Women Who Made Them* (Philadelphia, PA: J.B. Lippincott, 1929) Reprinted by EPM Publications, McLean, Virginia, 1992.

Fox, Sandi. *Quilts in Utah* (Salt Lake City: Salt Lake Arts Center, 1981).

Fox, Sandi. *Small Endearments* (New York: Charles Scribner's Sons, 1985).

Frank, Robert. *Frank's Art Needlework* of St. Louis was best known for its kits and stamped block sets, which they sold from about 1900 to 1980, but this is an unrelated Frank. Robert Frank Needlework Supply Company of Kalamazoo, MI, published at least one booklet:

E-Z Patterns for Patchwork and Applique Quilts

Gold-Art Needlework. A kit company.

Good Housekeeping. Periodical from the Hearst Corporation. Anne Orr was needlework editor in the early 20th century. See Anne Orr.

Gutcheon, Beth. *The Perfect Patchwork Primer* (New York: David McKay Co., 1973).

Hagerman, Betty J. *A Meeting of the Sunbonnet Children* (Baldwin, KS: By the author, 1979). Currently available from Mrs. Danner's Quilts. See Scioto Imhoff Danner.

Hall, Carrie A. and Rose G. Kretsinger. *The Romance of the Patchwork Quilt in America* (Caldwell, ID: Caxton Printers, 1935) Reprinted by Dover Publications, New York, NY.

Havig, Bettina. *Missouri Heritage Quilts* (Paducah, KY: American Quilter's Society, 1986).

Hearth and Home. Periodical published by Vickery and Hill Company in Augusta, Maine from 1885 to 1933. They offered their first mail order patterns in April, 1895. The company published many magazines that printed patterns. Among them: *American Woman, Fireside Visitor, Good Stories and Happy Hours*.

Herrschner. Frederick Herrschner, Inc. is a mail-order source for kits and stamped blocks dating back to the early twentieth century. They are still in business. One old booklet:

Quilts: Beautiful Designs for Applique, Embroidery: Authentic Reproductions for Patchwork.

Hinson, Delores A. *Quilting Manual* (New York: Hearthside Press, Inc, 1966) Reprinted by Dover Publications, New York, NY.

Hinson, Delores A., *A Quilter's Companion* (New York: Arco, 1973).

Holstein, Jonathan and Finley, John. *Kentucky Quilts: 1800-1900* (Louisville, KY: Kentucky Quilt Project, Inc., 1982).

Homeneedlecraft Creations. A kit company.

Horton, Laurel. *Social Fabric: South Carolina's Traditional Quilts* (Columbia, SC: McKissick Museum, University of SC, 1984).

Household, The. See *Capper's Weekly*.

Household Journal. Periodical published in Springfield, Ohio in the early 20th century by Crowell, which also published *Farm and Fireside*. Patterns were sold under the name Aunt Jane. *Household Journal* moved to Batavia, Illinois and was published as the *Household Management Journal*. Later absorbed by *Farm Journal*.

Pamphlets include:

> *Aunt Jane's Quilt Pattern Book*
> *Aunt Jane's Prize Winning Quilt Designs*
> (1914)

Ickis, Marguerite. *The Standard Book of Quilt Making and Collecting* (Grey Stone Press, 1949) Reprinted by Dover Publications, New York, NY, 1959.

Indiana Quilt Registry Project. *Quilts of Indiana* (Bloomington, Indiana: Indiana University Press, 1991).

Kansas City Star. Patterns appeared in three periodicals (*Kansas City Star*, *Weekly Kansas City Star* and *Weekly Star Farmer*) from 1928 to 1960. Early patterns were McKim syndicated patterns. In the 1930s the *Star* began a unique column of traditional and new designs by staff members and readers. Reprints available from Groves Quilt Patterns, PO Box 5370, Kansas City, MO 64131.

Kimball, Jeana. *Red and Green: An Applique Tradition* (Bothell, Washington: That Patchwork Place, 1990)

Ladies Art Company. Founded in St. Louis in 1889 by H.M. Brockstedt, it is credited as the first mail-order quilt pattern company. Exactly when they published their first catalog, *Diagrams of Quilt, Sofa and Pin Cushion Patterns*, has not been determined, but an 1895 ad mentions 272 patterns. The 1906 edition included 450 designs. A second catalog: *Quilt Patterns: Patchwork and Applique* was published in 1922 and revised again between 1928 and 1934 with patterns through 531. This last catalog was published until the company went out of business in the 1970s. Pattern historians Cuesta Benberry and Wilene Smith note that the number of the pattern can be used to date it. Applique designs from the 1920s were usually numbered in four digits. Following is an index to dates and three-digit numbers drawn from Wilene Smith's research, published as

"Quilt History in Old Periodicals: A New Interpretation," Uncoverings, 1990, Laurel Horton (ed.). (San Francisco: The American Quilt Study Group, 1991).

LAC Pattern Number	Date Published In print in 1895
1-272	(may date from 1889)
273-400	1897
401-420	1901
421-450	1906
451-500	1922
501-509	1928
511-530	1928-1934
531	1934

Ladies Home Journal. Periodical begun as *Ladies Journal and Practical Housekeeper* in 1883. Has published patterns until the present. Marie Webster contributed a number of patterns in the first quarter of the century.

Lady's Circle Patchwork Quilts. Periodical published by Lopez Publications since 1973. 111 E. 35th St., New York, New York, 10016.

Lasansky, Jeannette. *In the Heart of Pennsylvania: 19th and 20th Century Quiltmaking Traditions* (Lewisburg, PA: Oral Traditions Project, 1985).

Lasansky, Jeannette. *Pieced by Mother: Over 100 Years of Quiltmaking Tradition* (Lewisburg, PA: Oral Traditions Project, 1987).

Lockport Batting Company, Lockport, New York. In addition to selling supplies the company sold patterns during the 1930s and '40s. Lockport sold many Anne Orr designs (see entry.)

Booklets include:

> *Replicas of Famous Quilts, Old and New*, 1942
> *The Lockport Quilt Pattern Book*

MacDowell, Marsha and Fitzgerald, Ruth D. *Michigan Quilts: 150 Years of a Textile Tradition* (East Lansing, MI: Michigan State Museum, 1987).

McCall's Needlework. McCall's has sold patterns throughout the twentieth century via the pattern company and two periodicals, *McCall's Magazine* and *McCall's Needlework*.

McElwain, Mary A. The Mary McElwain Quilt Shop in Walworth, Wisconsin sold mail-order patterns in the 1930s, and some were included as premiums in batting.

One booklet:

> *The Romance of Village Quilts, 1936* (later reprinted by Rock River Cotton Co., Janesville, WI, ca. 1955)

McKim, Ruby Short. McKim Studios in Independence, Missouri was a mail-order source for patterns. She also syndicated a newspaper column with full-size patterns in the 1920s and 1930s.

Booklets:

> *Designs Worth Doing*
> *Adventures in Needlecraft*
> *Adventures in Home Beautifying*
> *101 Patchwork Patterns* (reprinted by Dover Publications, New York, New York, 1962)

Marston, Gwen and Joe Cunningham. *American Beauties: Rose and Tulip Quilts* (Paducah, Kentucky: American Quilter's Society, 1988).

L.K. Meeker. *Quilt Patterns for the Collector* (Portland, OR: by the author, 1979).

Modern Priscilla. Periodical begun in 1887 that offered mail-order patterns, primarily from 1910-1930. Absorbed by *Needlecraft–The Home Arts Magazine* (see entry) in 1930.

Mountain Mist. The Stearns & Foster Co. began selling quilt batting in Cincinnati in 1846. It has offered mail-order patterns at least since the 1920s when the company began including a free pattern on the batting wrapper. Phoebe Edwards is one of the names used. Address: Stearns & Foster Co. Lockland, OH 45215.

Booklets include:

> *The Moutain Mist Blue Book of Quilts,* 1935
> *The Mountain Mist Album of Quilt Blocks,* 1938
> *The 1957 Mountain Mist Blue Book of Quilts*
> *Anyone Can Quilt,* 1975
> *Stearns & Foster Catalogue of Quilt Pattern Designs and Needlecraft Supplies* (currently in print)

Needlecraft Magazine. This periodical was begun by Vickery and Hill Publishing Company in Augusta, Maine in 1909. The name changed several times. Among them: *Needlecrafts/The Home Arts Magazine* and *Home-Arts/Needlecraft*. It absorbed *Modern Priscilla* in 1930 and ceased publication in 1943.

Oklahoma Farmer Stockman. Periodical published in Oklahoma City. About 1930 it carried a unique column titled "Good Cheer Quilt Patterns."

Orlofsky, Myron & Patsy Orlofsky. *Quilts in America* (New York: McGraw Hill, 1974) Reprinted by Abbeville Press, 1992.

Orr, Anne. A designer of quilt and other needlework patterns in the early twentieth century and a needlework editor at *Good Housekeeping Magazine*. Anne Orr patterns were sold under her name, *Good Housekeeping*'s and the Lockport Batting Company's name.

Page, Nancy. A syndicated mail-order column written by Florence LaGanke Harris, which appeared in many periodicals from 1928 through the 1930s. She specialized in appliqued, series designs.

Paragon. A kit company, apparently still in business. Kits marketed through magazines and in catalogs such as Herrschners.

Penny, Prudence. The name for the column in the *Seattle Post-Intelligencer* in the 1920s and 1930s. The author was Bernice Redington, the paper's food editor.

Booklet:

> *Old Time Quilts,* 1927

People's Popular Monthly. A periodical published from 1896 to 1931, which absorbed *Ladies' Favorite Magazine* in 1908.

Peterson's Magazine. A periodical begun in 1842 as *Lady's World of Fashion*. The owners changed the name in 1849 and merged with Argosy in 1894. Occasionally showed quilt patterns.

Peto, Florence, *American Quilts and Coverlets* (New York: Chanticleer Press, Inc., 1949).

Peto, Florence, *Historic Quilts* (New York: American Historical Co., Inc., 1939).

Progress. A kit company, apparently still in business. Kits marketed through magazines and in catalogs.

Quilt Engagement Calendar. An annual desk calendar edited by Cyril Nelson from E.P. Dutton, published from 1975 to the present. Patterns for several quilts in Cyril I. Nelson's and Carter Houck's, *The Quilt Engagement Treasury* (New York: E.P. Dutton, 1982).

Quilters Newsletter Magazine. Periodical published since 1969, edited by Bonnie Leman. Address: PO Box 394, Wheatridge, CO 80033. Includes a mail-order pattern service called Quilts and Other Comforts, once known as Heirloom Plastics.

Rainbow. A company begun by William Pinch in Cleveland in the 1920s. Rainbow is best known for its stamped blocks for embroidery, but also sold applique kits in block form. Most of the patterns indexed here are applique combined with embroidery. Current address: Rainbow Quilts, Box 15126, Plantation, FL 33318.

Ramsey, Bets and Waldvogel, Merikay. *Quilts of Tennessee: Images of Domestic Life Prior to 1930* (Nashville: Rutledge Hill Press, 1986).

Roan, Nancy. *Just A Quilt/Juscht En Deppich* (Green Lane, Pennsylvania: Goschenhoppen Historians, 1984).

Roberson, Ruth Haslip (ed.). *North Carolina Quilts* (Chapel Hill: University of North Carolina Press, 1988).

Rural New Yorker. A periodical begun in 1841 and published through the mid-twentieth century. Mrs. R.E. Smith wrote an apparently unique pattern column from 1930 through 1937. She mentioned once that the column was syndicated, but I have not seen it elsewhere.

Safford, Carleton L. and Robert Bishop. *America's Quilts and Coverlets* (New York: E.P. Dutton, 1972).

St. Louis Fancywork Company. An art needlework company that sold quilt patterns as Martha Washington Patchwork. The designers were Amy Conway and Sophie T. LaCroix.

One pamphlet:

> *Martha Washington Patchwork*, 1916

Sears, Roebuck & Co. *Century of Progress in Quilt Making.* Chicago, 1934. Booklet featuring winners of their contest held in conjunction with the 1933 World's Fair.

Sexton, Carlie. Carlie Sexton Holmes ran a mail-order patterns company from Wheaton, Illinois in the late 1920s and 1930s. She also wrote for Meredith Corporation, publisher of *Successful Farming* and *Better Homes & Gardens.*

Booklets:

> *Old Fashioned Quilts* (Wheaton, IL: By the author, 1928)
> *Yesterday's Quilts in Homes of Today* (Des Moines, IA: Meredith Publishing, 1928)
> *How To Make a Quilt* (Wheaton, IL: By the author, 1932)

Shelburne Museum, Shelburne, Vermont.

Two catalogs:

> Lillian Baker Carlisle. *Pieced Work and Applique Quilts at Shelburne Museum* (Shelburne, VT: Shelburne Museum, 1957)
> Celia Y. Oliver. *55 Famous Quilts from the Shelburne Museum* (Shelburne, VT: Shelburne Museum, 1991)

Sienkiewicz, Elly. *Spoken Without a Word, A Lexicon of Symbols with Twenty-Four Patterns from the Baltimore Album Quilts,* (Washington, D.C.: By the author, 1983).

Sienkiewicz, Elly. *Baltimore Beauties and Beyond, Studies in Classic Album Quilt Applique, Vol. I and II* (Lafayette, CA: C & T Publishing, 1989 and 1990).

Spencer Museum of Art, University of Kansas.

Three catalogs:

> *One Hundred Years of American Quilts* (Lawrence, KS: Spooner-Thayer Museum, 1973)
> *Quilters Choice* (Lawrence, KS: Helen F. Spencer Museum of Art, 1978)
> *American Patchwork Quilt* (Tokyo: Kokusai Art, 1988)

Successful Farming. Periodical published by Meredith Corporation, Des Moines, Iowa; begun in 1902 and continued through the middle of this century. See Carlie Sexton.

Texas Heritage Quilt Society. *Texas Quilts, Texas Treasures* (Paducah, KY: American Quilter's Society, 1986).

Uncoverings. The annual papers of the American Quilt Study Group, San Francisco. 660 Mission St., Suite 400, San Francisco, CA 94105.

Vickery Publishing. Company also known as Vickery and Hill from Augusta, Maine. Vickery published several periodicals and many quilt patterns. See *Hearth and Home.*

Webster, Marie D. *Quilts: Their Story And How To Make Them* (New York: Tudor Publishing Co., 1915) Reprint from Practical Patchwork, Santa Barbara, CA, 1990. Webster also wrote for the *Ladies Home Journal* and sold patterns from her home in Indiana.

Wheeler, Laura or Alice Brooks. Names used by Needlecraft Service, a mail-order company begun in 1933 that continues to advertise in periodicals, although most of their quilt patterns are no longer offered. Other names include Carol Curtis and Reader Mail. Until recently their address was the Old Chelsea Station post office in New York City. Current address: Reader Mail, Box 4000, Niles, MI 49120-4000.

Booklets include:

> *Quilt Book #101*
> *Museum Quilt Book #102*
> *Quilts for Today's Living #103*
> *Nifty Fifty Quilts #116, 1974*
> *Stuff 'n' Puff Quilts #122*
> *Stitch 'n Patch Quilts #123*
> *Petal Quilt Book #125*

Woman's Day. Periodical that has included quilt patterns from the 1940s to the present. Some of the articles were reprinted in Rose Wilder Lane's *Woman's Day Book of American Needlework* (New York: Simon & Schuster, 1962).

Woman's Home Companion. Periodical that began in 1866 as *Ladies Home Companion* and changed its name in 1899.

Woman's World. Periodical published by the Manning Publlishing Company, Chicago in the 1920s and 30s.

Booklet:

> *The Patchwork Book*, 1931

Woodard, Thomas K. and Blanche Greenstein. *Crib Quilts and Other Small Wonders* (New York: E.P. Dutton, 1981).

Woodard, Thomas K. and Blanche Greenstein. *Twentieth Century Quilts 1900-1950* (New York: E.P. Dutton, 1988).

Workbasket, The. Periodical begun in 1935 as a leaflet by Colonial Patterns, Inc. (see Aunt Martha). It was affiliated with the Aunt Martha Studios until 1949 when Workbasket and Colonial Patterns split and Modern Handcrafts began publishing *The Workbasket*. After 1950 the magazine rarely published quilt patterns, but has recently published some reprints.

Alphabetical Index to Names

Decorative Plant, 41.93

Delphinium, 21.32

Delphiniums, 33.81

Democrat Rose, 18.24, 18.35, 20.92

Democratic Rose, 12.84, 18.5, 41.99

Des Moines Rose, 3.7

Desert Bell Flower, 32.93

Diamond Vine, 20.97

Dianthus, 36.58

Dickey Bird, 52.3

Dickie, 49.86

Dixie Rose, 33.32

Dog Applique, 55.55

Doggie Applique, 55.54

Dogwood, 9.92, 21.14, 22.34, 32.11, 32.13, 34.75, 82.994, 82.997

Dogwood Basket, 80.13

Dogwood Beauty, 82.998

Dolly Varden, 82.91

Dotty, 49.85

Double Dahlia, 14.26, 20.22

Double Heart, 9.843

Double Hearts, 14.95, 24.4

Double Irish Cross, 9.812

Double Peony & Wild Rose, 12.93

Double Poppy, 9.921, 27.81

Double Tulip, 12.93, 37.12

Dove Applique, 52.12

Dream Ship, 59.24

Dresden Plate, 27.3

Ducky Coverlet, 53.35

Ducky Doo, 53.44

Dutch Boy, 48.17, 49.63, 85.27

Dutch Boy & Girl, 49.68

Dutch Girl, 47.48, 85.26

Dutch Girls, 49.62

Dutch Lass, 49.61

Dutch Roses, 39.25

Dutch Tulip, 8.33, 28.13

Dutch Tulips, 29.52

Dutch Tulip Basket, 42.77

Eagle Applique, 54.7

Early American, 89.2

Early Rose of Sharon, 31.82

Early to Bed, 49.78

Early Tulips, 29.964, 29.99

Easter Lilies, 22.85

Eastern Star, 60.71

Edith Hall's Rose, 13.43

Egyptian Lotus, 42.93

Egyptian Lotus Flower, 41.56

Eight of Hearts, 9.842

Eight Pointed Star w/Sprigs, 14.83

Elderberry Bloom, 12.37

Elephant, 56.42, 56.45, 56.47

Elephant's Child, 86.8

Emporia Rose, 36.25

Enchanted Cottage, 58.16

English Flower Garden, 39.24

English Garden, 39.24

English Rose, 12.88

Esther's Plume, 36.73

Evening Flower Block, 32.52

Evergreen Tree, 57.7

Falling Leaves, 71.3

Family Tree, 88.3

Fancy Butterfly, 51.14

Farmer Boy, 48.24, 48.7

Farmer's Barometer, 25.3

Feather, 19.62

Feather Crown, 1.12

Feather Crown w/Ragged Robin, 1.13

Feather Flower, 37.99

Feather Rose, 15.22, 36.75

Festoon Quilt, 90.4

Field Daisy, 26.53

Field Flowers, 33.59, 37.59

Firefly, 51.4

Fireworks, 10.89

First Lady, 81.63

Fisher Boy, 48.54

Garland & Basket, 80.47
Garland of Leaves, 1.64
Gay Butterflies, 51.35
Gay Garden, 45.82
Gay Print Pansy, 37.65
Gay Tulips, 8.56
Geneva Tassal Flower, 9.945
Geometrical Rose, 36.38
Geranium, 39.34
Geranium Wreath, 12.35
Giant Primrose, 34.68
Gift of Love, 60.56
Gingham Bush, 39.9
Gladiola, 82.73
Globe Thistle, 32.57
Golden Bells, 8.92
Golden Butterflies. . ., 86.15
Golden Corn, 9.73
Golden Lily, 35.23
Golden Poppies, 42.85
Golden Rose of Virginia, 31.1
Goldenrod, 21.26
Good Luck Block, 9.821
Good Luck Clover, 9.1, 9.822
Gorgeous Pansies, 37.664
Grandmother's Dream, 9.32
Grandmother's Engagement Ring, 25.9
Grandmother's Flower Quilt, 29.26
Grandmother's Garden, 73.7
Grandmother's Prize Quilt, 39.55
Grandmother's Quilt, 11.832
Grandmother's Sunbonnet, 27.12
Grandmother's Sunburst, 27.12
Grape & Morning Glory, 16.3
Grape Wreath, 2.13
Grapes, 1.57, 46.83
Grapes & Oak Leaf, 16.67
Grapes & Vines, 26.94
Grapevine Block, 9.63
Great Divide, 91.1

Hallo Een Quilt, 85.5
Hallowe'en Block, 50.8

Happy Jack, 48.6
Harebells, 8.87
Harrison Rose, 17.32, 31.25, 31.26
Harvest Rose, 18.74
Hawaiian Blocks, 9.76
Hawaiian Flower, 4.1
Hawthorne Berries, 16.1
Heart & Dove, 52.92
Heart & Spade, 52.92
Heart for Applique, 9.874
Hearts, 9.825, 11.12, 24.5
Hearts All Around, 9.85
Hearts & Diamonds, 24.82, 24.86
Hearts & Flowers, 11.23, 21.72, 26.86,
    42.995, 72.6
Heirloom Historic Quilt, 33.18
Hero's Crown, 17.21
Hibiscus, 35.25, 35.27
Hickory Leaf, 17.11, 17.13
Hobby Horse, 56.58
Holland Tulip, 21.56
Holly Hocks, 90.33
Holly Leaves, 5.22
Holly Wreath, 1.55
Hollyhock, 33.56, 35.46
Hollyhock Wreath, 2.53
Homestead, 58.17
Honey Bee, 5.33
Honeysuckle, 10.84, 16.4
Hop Vine, 43.24
Horn of Plenty, 38.22, 38.23, 38.24, 38.32,
    38.34, 38.4, 73.82
Horse Chestnut, 21.36
Hospitality, 9.77
House & Hill, 58.3
Humoristic Cat & Dog, 55.28
Hunter's Horn, 45.79

Indian Paint Brush, 2.74
Indian Princess, 49.35
Indian Princess Feather, 36.73
Indiana Rose, 8.73, 12.65
Indiana Wreath, 80.22, 80.23

Initial Quilt, 82.98
Iowa Rose, 3.7
Iowa Rose Wreath, 4.33
Ipswich Bouquet, 14.72
Iris, 22.54, 26.67, 26.68, 26.69, 37.72,
   37.742, 37.743, 37.75, 37.79, 82.75, 82.76
Iris in Baskets, 42.91
Irish Beauty, 12.95
Irish Chain, 17.12
Irish Rose, 11.88
Irish Shamrock, 35.5
Ivory Basket, 42.758
Ivy, 32.41

Jack Rabbit, 56.35
Jasmine, 34.56
Jefferson Rose, 12.14
Jersey Bouquet, 12.71
Jersey Rose, 12.71
Jerusalem Cross, 45.85
Jester's Plume, 19.44
Job's Patience, 17.11
Job's Tears, 5.13
Jonah's Fish, 56.62
Jonquils, 22.62, 37.85, 42.24
June Basket, 80.24
June Lily, 29.45
June Rose, 20.38
Just Ducky, 53.42

Kansas Pattern, 45.42
Kansas Sunflower, 27.24, 27.85, 37.917
Keepsake Quilt, 85.31
Kentucky Columbine, 34.22
Kentucky Peony, 37.213
Kentucky Rose, 2.31, 2.63, 19.17, 45.26
Kiddies' Ride, 85.17
King's Crown, 9.943
Kitten, 56.11, 56.12, 56.14, 56.15, 56.17

Ladies Art Company, 6082, 38.25
Ladies' Dream, 14.843

Lady Delano, 82.17
Lady Sheridan, 80.16
Lamb, 56.55
Landon Sunflower, 27.14
Larkspur, 34.24
Laurel Leaves, 5.55, 21.22
Laurel Wreath, 72.5
Lavender Lace Flower, 14.79
Lavender Puzzle, 20.98
Leaf Quilt, 5.18, 71.5
Leaves in the Wind, 25.7
Lemon Lily, 23.3
Lilac Zinnia, 9.983
Lilacs, 25.6
Lilies of France, 21.86
Lilies of the Valley, 32.83
Lily, 4.87, 29.84, 35.22, 37.36
Lily Basket, 42.55
Lily of the Valley, 8.12, 8.18, 29.83, 32.76,
   32.85
Lily Pond, 37.34
Little Bowser, 55.53
Little Brown Koko, 74.6
Little Chanticlear, 53.14
Little Dutch Boy, 49.66
Little Dutch Girl, 47.17
Little Jumbo, 56.43
Little Man in the Moon, 85.11
Little Miss Tiptoe, 85.21
Little Omar, 56.54
Little Red Riding Hood, 85.44
Little Village, 58.17
Lobster, 6.7
Lombardy Lily, 8.47
Loretta's Rose, 8.66
Lotus Blossom, 37.313, 41.19
Lotus Bud, 8.71
Lotus Flower, 8.61, 25.23, 33.25
Louisiana Rose, 11.62, 11.62b
Love Apple, 46.61, 46.62, 46.63, 46.64
Love in the Mist, 27.5
Love Rose, 33.12

Luck Quilt, 9.821
Lucky Elephant, 56.48

Magic Vine, 90.31
Magnolia Applique, 37.31
Magnolia Blooms, 82.84
Magnolia Buds in Floral Maze, 9.52
Magyar Flower Pot, 39.36
Mahoning Rose, 19.15
Maple Leaf, 5.73, 37.11
March Tulip, 21.92
Marie Antoinette, 82.21
Marigold, 17.35
Marigolds, 32.58
Martha Washington Wreath, 2.66
Martha's Vineyard, 16.55
Marvel of Peru, 35.49
Mary Ann, 47.24
Mary Lou, 47.26
Mary Moore's Double Irish Chain, 9.812
Maude Hare's Basket, 42.745
Maude Hare's Flower Garden, 46.16
May Basket, 42.72, 42.743
Meadow Daisy, 22.32, 22.44
Meadow Rose, 32.12, 36.89
Melon Patch, 13.32
Memory Block, 12.72
Memory Bouquet, 73.4
Mexican Rose, 21.46, 22.12, 22.13, 22.15,
    22.41, 22.42, 36.33
Mexican Rosebud, 22.66
Mexican Shell Flower, 33.64
Mexican Tea Rose, 20.37
Midnight Sky, 10.89
Mignonette, 33.74
Mimosa Wreath, 14.71
Missouri Rose, 44.7
Mistress Betty, 85.22
Modern Corsage, 9.923
Modern Flower Block, 33.76
Modern Pineapple, 46.41
Modern Poinsettia, 37.924

Modern Wild Rose, 34.48
Modernistic Flower, 72.7
Monday's Trees, 57.94
Moon Blossoms, 7.6
Moonflower, 3.2, 34.31
Morning Glories, 51.66, 81.77
Morning Glories in a Circle, 37.49
Morning Glory, 4.55, 9.55, 9.57, 9.58, 34.42,
    34.69, 36.57, 37.42, 37.43, 37.46, 81.73,
    81.75, 82.63, 82.65, 82.992
Morning Glory Net, 26.75
Morning Glory Vine Scroll, 82.66
Moss Rose, 36.83, 37.293
Mother Goose, 53.72, 74.17, 74.4, 85.33
Mountain Laurel, 19.37, 20.14
Mountain Lily, 29.25
Mountain Star, 27.62
Mr. Owl, 52.74
Mrs. Brown's Peony, 22.2
Mrs. Hall's Basket, 42.717
Mrs. Harris's Colonial Rose, 13.41
Mrs. Kretsinger's Rose, 14.65
Muscatel Grape, 1.56

Narcissus, 36.14, 37.81, 37.87
Nasturtium, 36.16
Nasturtium Wreath, 4.84
Nasturtiums, 42.25
Nebraska Oak Leaf, 17.33
New Jersey Rose, 12.71
New Rose of Sharon, 11.75
New Tulip Block, 11.92
Newark Wreath, 2.69
Noah's Ark, 86.71, 86.72
North Across the Border, 88.4
North Carolina Lily, 37.14
North Carolina Rose, 2.33, 25.22
Nosegay, 39.15
Nursery Patch, 56.16

Oak Leaf, 5.72, 16.64, 17.11, 17.20, 17.24,
    17.73, 19.18, 19.22, 23.12, 23.17, 43.22

Petunias, 35.7
Philadelphia Beauty, 6.2
Phillipsburg (PA) Flower Pot, 39.6
Pieced Pineapple, 46.47
Pilot's Wheel, 1.69
Pine Tree, 21.24
Pineapple, 9.75, 17.51, 46.41, 46.42, 46.44, 46.45
Piney, 9.34
Pink Dogwood in Baskets, 80.44
Pink Rose, 45.23
Pinks, 18.14
Pinwheel Bouquet, 27.87
Plain Butterfly, 51.16
Planet Jupiter, 13.54
Plymouth Garden, 82.88
Poinsettia, 9.36, 16.66, 20.96, 21.13, 26.63, 33.13, 33.52, 33.87, 37.923, 80.49
Poke Berries, 43.52
Pomegranate, 9.67, 12.22, 12.26, 12.28, 14.848, 46.74
Pompom, 5.15, 32.59
Poplar Leaf, 6.1
Poppies, 37.551, 37.56, 37.58
Poppy, 17.36, 19.72, 37.51, 37.555, 45.34, 81.23, 82.42, 82.46, 82.48
Poppy Basket, 80.34, 80.42
Poppy Field, 37.544
Poppy Garden, 37.546, 37.548
Poppy Wreath, 82.41
Portulaca, 20.42
Posies Around the Square, 25.86
Pot of Flowers, 39.52, 39.53
Pot of Poppies, 40.15
Pot of Tulips, 39.45
Potted Rose, 42.642
Potted Rose Bush, 29.86
Potted Tulip, 41.551
Prairie Pinks, 35.6
Prairie Flower, 44.6, 44.7
Prairie Rose, 11.52, 44.1
President's Wreath, 2.65, 2.72, 2.76

Pretty Snowflake, 75.84
Prickly Pear, 17.52
Pride of Iowa, 41.552
Pride of the Forest, 43.48
Pride of the Garden, 28.2
Primrose, 1.37, 34.68
Primrose Wreath, 4.82
Prince's Feather, 10.78, 23.4
Princess Feather, 5.52, 15.12, 15.18, 15.24, 15.4, 15.54, 36.74, 36.77
Princess Feather & Tulip, 19.35
Princess Feather with Oak Leaves, 15.52
Princess Feathers, 15.16, 15.3
Priscilla Alden, 36.18
Priscilla's Poppies, 37.57
Provincial, 82.81
Pumpkin, 12.68
Pumpkin Blossom, 14.844
Puppies, 55.56
Puppy, 55.42, 55.51
Purple Iris, 37.76
Pussy Cat, 75.12

Quilt of Birds, 73.13, 75.62

Radical Rose, 11.72
Ragged Robin, 17.35
Rainbow Quilt, 37.88
Rambling Rose, 44.8
Rappahannock Rose, 31.34
Rare Old Tulip, 29.44, 29.49, 29.55
Recollect, 48.28
Red Bird, 52.26
Red Hot Poker, 5.15
Red Oak Block, 19.23
Red Peony, 37.17
Red Poppies, 37.553
Red Sails, 59.13
Reel, 17.11
Regal Lily, 29.43
Remember, 47.28
Rio Wreath, 21.94

JON GIERLICH

About the Author

Barbara Brackman became interested in quilt patterns as an undergraduate at the University of Kansas in the 1960s. At the back of the classroom in which she studied art history, she discovered drawers full of quilt blocks. They were the collection of Carrie Hall who had published a patchwork index in the 1930s, *The Romance of the Patchwork Quilt in America*.

Determined to make a quilt in every design, Barbara started a file of quilt blocks. She soon realized, as Carrie Hall had, that one person could not hope to stitch a block in every pattern, much less a quilt. An index card on each, however, was possible; and over the past 25 years her file has grown to include thousands of quilt patterns.

In the 1980s Barbara published, and continued to augment, an *Encyclopedia of Pieced Quilt Patterns*. Out of her dedicated research in pattern identification grew a knowledge of two centuries of quilt style, fabric, technique and design that led in 1989 to her much-acclaimed book, *Clues in the Calico: A Guide to Identifying and Dating Antique Quilts*. She also has co-authored several books on quilt history including *Kansas Quilts and Quilters* with members of the Kansas Quilt Project and *Patchwork Souvenirs of the 1933 World's Fair* with Merikay Waldvogel. Now her computer is replacing her card files and she is at work computerizing both her pieced and applique indexes. Her original encyclopedia of pieced patterns has been re-issued by the American Quilter's Society to coincide with the much-awaited publication of the book at hand, *Encyclopedia of Applique*.

Barbara Brackman divides her time between Lawrence, Kansas, and Seattle, Washington. She teaches workshops in quiltmaking and dating and identifying antique quilts. She also curates museum exhibits and is well known for her articles in *Quilter's Newsletter Magazine*, *Americana* and the American Quilt Study Group's *Uncoverings*.